Introduction to
Professional Practice

*A Student Text/Workbook Designed to
Enhance the Cooperative Education Experience*
Third Edition

University of Cincinnati
Division of Professional Practice

**McGraw-Hill Primis
Custom Publishing**

Boston   Burr Ridge, IL   Dubuque, IA   Madison, WI   New York   San Francisco   St. Louis
Bangkok   Bogotá   Caracas   Lisbon   London   Madrid
Mexico City   Milan   New Delhi   Seoul   Singapore   Sydney   Taipei   Toronto

McGraw-Hill Higher Education
A Division of The McGraw-Hill Companies

Introduction to
Professional Practice
A Student Text/Workbook Designed to Enhance the Cooperative Education Experience

Copyright © 2001, 1999, 1996 by The McGraw-Hill Companies, Inc. All rights reserved. Printed in the United States of America. Except as permitted under the United States Copyright Act of 1976, no part of this publication may be reproduced or distributed in any form or by any means, or stored in a data base retrieval system, without prior written permission of the publisher.

McGraw-Hill's Primis Custom Series consists of products that are produced from camera-ready copy. Peer review, class testing, and accuracy are primarily the responsibility of the author(s).

8 9 0 OFC OFC 9 8 7 6 5 4 3 2 1

ISBN 0-07-252394-8

Sponsoring Editor: Jan Scipio
Cover Design and students photo: Lauren K. Adair
Photo: Employers. Copyright © 1990 Ron Chapple
Printer/Binder: Ohio Full Court Press

Table of Contents

Preface

Section One ■ Overview of Cooperative Education
Chapter 1
    The History of Cooperative Education 3

Chapter 2
    Learning through Cooperative Education 25

Section Two ■ Components of the Job Search
Chapter 3
    Career Planning 45

Chapter 4
    Goal Setting 77

Chapter 5
    Guidelines for Resume Preparation 89

Chapter 6
    The Portfolio 119

Chapter 7
    Interviewing 125

Section Three ■ Routes to Success on the Co-op Job and Beyond
Chapter 8
    Surviving and Thriving on the Job 151

Chapter 9
    Networking: Using People in the Best Sense 177

Chapter 10
    Responding to the Reality of a Transcultural World 181

Chapter 11
    Sexual Harassment 189

References 200

About the Contributors 203

PREFACE

As cooperative education heads toward its 100th anniversary in 2006, several developments are taking place in the field. I believe that Herman Schneider, past University of Cincinnati Dean of Engineering and the founder of cooperative education (co-op) in 1906, would be pleased with many of the developments that are taking place. There is a strong movement toward adhering to minimum operational and educational standards for co-op programs from organizations and accrediting bodies. The addition of co-op accrediting bodies and return to former co-op methods has contributed to a refinement of programs categorized as "co-op;" however, it has led to a new and dynamic discussion which promotes all experiential education. Another development has taken place in the academy, itself. Many institutions have been taking an inventory of their own student and general education programs in an effort to improve and enhance learning, and co-op has been affected. While institutions have been refining and improving their co-op programs to meet these new demands, a healthy economic climate has facilitated continued employer participation as student hirers and field organizers. The Co-op Triad—the student, the employer, and the university—continues in the tradition in which Herman Schneider first conceived it.

In addition to cooperative education programs of many models, there are internship, service learning, work/study, school-to-work and other experiential education methods. Curriculum-related work experience continues to be a developing educational method in college institutions, as well as, in middle and high schools. There are nearly seven hundred college-level cooperative education programs in the United States and internationally, and many more for students aged 15 to 18. Hundreds of thousands of students and employers participate in these programs. Through these experiential education programs, teaching institutions are providing students with work experiences in virtually every field and industry.

An important step in delivering a quality experiential education program is preparing students for effective participation. The University of Cincinnati faculty has developed a text/workbook that makes this step both structured and uncomplicated. *Introduction to Professional Practice: A Student Text/Workbook Designed to Enhance the Cooperative Education Experience* was developed to prepare students for participation in cooperative education (co-op) and other discipline and career-related experiential education programs. The text is written for co-op practitioners and advisers who feel the need to develop or strengthen their "Intro to Co-op'" preparation courses and seminars. A good preparatory course for cooperative education students can be a critical element in the success of an institution's co-op program. Because of the effect that a preparatory course can have on a co-op program, the course developer will need to plan carefully.

The text has examples of tools that can be used for documenting student learning and achievements. It also has several case studies of actual student situations and dilemmas while on co-op. When used in conjunction with the institutions' rules and policies for student participation, the text will offer a wealth of opportunities for any Intro to Co-op course.

Introduction to Professional Practice will help students reflect on and articulate learning by:
1. helping them to work with school coordinators and employment supervisors to set realistic learning objectives;

2. providing them with instructional tools and forms that help document work experience;
3. helping them to understand the work conditions by which learning can be optimized; and
4. giving them an awareness of what can be learned while on co-op.

It will help students prepare for the job search by:
1. assisting them with self-assessment of their skills and interest;
2. familiarizing them with career and company research methods;
3. teaching them how to develop an effective resume, and
4. preparing them for the interview process.

Co-op professors and workshop facilitators will find *Introduction to Professional Practice: A Student Text/Workbook Designed to Enhance the Cooperative Education Experience* to be a valuable resource in preparing students for school related work. Students will find it easy to comprehend and text to which they can refer long after they have completed their course and throughout their co-op experiences.

> Darnice R. Langford
> Associate Professor of Professional Practice
> University of Cincinnati

SECTION ONE

Overview of Cooperative Education

Education is a social process...Education is growth...
Education is not a preparation for life;
Education is life itself.

–John Dewey

CHAPTER ONE

The History of Cooperative Education

A young man, to achieve, must first get out of his mind any notion either of the ease or rapidity of success...Nothing ever just happens in this world: Everything is brought about. Success never comes to a man of its own volition: It will meet a man halfway, but it will never come to him all the way.

—Edward W. Bok

For today's problems are *age-old in essence;
only the setting and the details vary.*
–Herman Schneider

"Cooperative Education" is the formal integration of classroom theory (academic education) with work experience (practical education). This method of education was designed to expand, enhance, and enrich the student's college academic training.

Cooperative education was conceived and developed by Herman Schneider, a Professor of Engineering at the University of Cincinnati, at the beginning of the twentieth century. Schneider, who later became Dean of Engineering and then President of the University of Cincinnati, believed that his students would learn engineering better if their curriculum was enhanced by his plan to integrate theory and practice throughout their academic training. The heart of his plan was to have students alternate a week of classroom study with a week of on-the-job discipline/career-related work experiences.

Schneider began promoting his plan in 1899, but getting acceptance was not an easy task. Cincinnati industrialists thought that college students weren't suited for working in the "rough" environment of the manufacturing shop. At the same time, the University academicians thought that Schneider's proposed cooperative education program would not be sufficiently "academic" to produce a well-educated individual.

It took Herman Schneider seven years to convince both his faculty colleagues and Cincinnati industrialists to support this new educational concept. Even so, the members of the University of Cincinnati Board of Trustees were cautious: in 1906, in a split vote, the Board gave one-year, trial approval to the cooperative education plan. Cooperative education was launched with 27 students and 13 "cooperative" employers.

From this modest beginning, cooperative education–the "Cincinnati Plan" as it was called-has grown to include more than 900 post-secondary institutions, 195,000 students, and 80,000 employers throughout the United States and abroad. Roughly one-third of the nation's post-secondary education institutions have some form of cooperative education program.

While cooperative education originated with the academic discipline of engineering, today virtually every higher education major and discipline is represented in a co-op program somewhere in the United States or internationally. Over the years, cooperative education has developed numerous variations on the original alternating one-week model. There are now programs that alternate by terms, quarters, semesters, and on a variety of other college and university schedules. There are also co-op experiences that operate as parallel programs, where students work part of a day or week and are also enrolled either full-time or part-time in their academic classes. Today's cooperative education programs are flourishing in all types of educational settings: two-year, four-year, and five-year baccalaureate programs; masters programs; and vocational and traditional secondary schools.

The Co-op Triad

Co-op education is based on a tripartite partnership between the co-op employer, the student, and the university, including the academic faculty and the co-op faculty/advisers.

A successful cooperative education program depends on the involvement and supportive interdependence of each member in the triad. Each member of the partnership has a well-defined and critical role to play.

The Co-op Triad

University/College/Faculty Role

In higher education co-op programs, the primary responsibility of the co-op faculty/adviser is the education of the student. In most co-op programs, the college or department faculty have as their goal the successful integration of classroom theory with the practice that students receive through their discipline-related co-op work experiences.

In fulfilling their cooperative education responsibilities, co-op faculty/advisers:

1. Identify and develop discipline–or degree-related co-op work assignments and corporate co-op programs. This requires co-op faculty/advisers to

    ♦ have basic knowledge of the academic discipline

    ♦ know of current trends in the related career fields

    ♦ be familiar with the educational requirements for the related career fields

    ♦ monitor the co-op experience for degree relevancy

    ♦ assess the contribution of the co-op experience to the student's education and professional preparation

2. Meet regularly with assigned students after their co-op work assignments to

    ♦ assess the student performance during the work assignment

    ♦ help the student integrate co-op work assignments with classroom learning

    ♦ establish objectives for future co-op experiences and career goals

    ♦ grant credit or assign an appropriate grade

3. Work closely with faculty in the degree-granting colleges to

    ♦ establish an academic partnership

    ♦ insure the fulfillment of the overall academic mission for students

Employer Role

The employer has a critical role within the co-op triad. The employer must design work assignments that meet the company's objectives and that also satisfy the experiential needs of the student and the program needs of the university. As a result, although employers have basic bottom line needs, they also serve as educators. Employers facilitate student learning by:

1. Establishing company co-op programs and co-op positions that

    - offer discipline–or degree-related work assignments
    - designate an appropriate supervisor
    - provide a meaningful, even if tentative, job description
    - maintain open communication with the college/university
    - pay students a fair co-op salary
    - follow equal employment opportunity guidelines

2. Providing human resource management systems that

    - coordinate the co-op employment process (in most cases, employers select the students for work assignments)
    - conduct co-op performance appraisals
    - give periodic progress reports and advice
    - establish goals for the co-op employee
    - provide co-op employees with a basic orientation to the workplace
    - provide adequate instruction and training for specific work assignments

Student Role

The student's role in the co-op triad is to participate fully in learning from the co-op experience, both in the classroom and during work assignments. Student goals should focus on receiving the full benefit of the co-op learning opportunities.

1. As co-op employees, students are expected to

    - conduct themselves in a professional and productive manner
    - adhere to all company policies and procedures
    - seek advice and feedback from supervisor
    - take all opportunities to learn new tasks, activities and processes
    - discuss problems and concerns with the supervisor, human resources manager and/or co-op faculty representative

- keep a log, journal or other record of tasks, accomplishments and supervisor feedback
- attempt to find ways to apply classroom theory with practical experience

2. In the classroom, co-op students are expected to

- complete a report assessing the learning gained from the co-op assignment
- make continuous progress toward completion of their degree requirements
- attempt to find ways to integrate practice experience and classroom theory

One's work may be finished someday but one's education, never.
–Alexander Dumas, the Elder

Ethics for Co-op and for the Workplace

The strength of a triangle is its three stable sides. The cooperative education triad can only be as strong as any one of the three partners. The Cooperative Education Association has established a *Code of Ethics* to guide all members of the cooperative education triad. When put into practice, these principles benefit all those involved in the cooperative education process. These principles create a framework that helps co-op participants establish guidelines for professional conduct.

Principles for University Co-op Professionals

1. Cooperative education professionals are responsible for establishing and monitoring practices that ensure the fair and accurate representation of students and the co-op program to employers.

2. Co-op professionals should respect student rights covered by state/federal privacy laws.

3. Co-op professionals should promote and follow non-discriminatory practices.

4. Co-op professionals should promote the concept of cooperative education in general as well as promoting their own program.

5. Co-op professionals should strive to develop new work opportunities for their students rather than pursuing co-op positions developed by other institutions.

6. The right of the employer to choose employees based upon their credentials should be respected.

*If your only goal is to become rich,
you will never achieve it.*
–John D. Rockefeller

Principles for Co-op Employers

1. Employers are responsible for the ethical and legal conduct of their employees throughout the co-op process.

2. Employers should respect the legal obligations of co-op professionals and request only those services or information that can legally be provided.

3. Employers should not misrepresent positions offered.

4. Employers should honor the policies and procedures of colleges or universities.

5. Employers should not ask students to participate in any activities that are unethical or illegal.

6. Employers should consider the long-range career plans of the individual student as opposed to the immediate needs of the company before extending offers of full-time employment before the student has completed his/her education.

7. Employer co-op professionals should make every effort to honor offers of co-op employment once they have been formally extended.

Principles for Co-op Students

1. Students should honor the policies of their college or university as well as the personnel policies of their employers.

2. Students should present their qualifications and interests as accurately as possible when interviewing for co-op positions.

3. Students should interview only if there is sincere interest in the co-op position.

4. Students should notify employers of acceptance/rejection of offers as soon as possible.

5. After accepting an offer, a student should withdraw from the job search process and notify the university as well as other employers from whom offers may be pending.

Differences Between Co-op and Other Work

Critics (or the uninformed) say, "Students can get the same experience on their own."

Not true. According to the William T. Grant Commission on Youth and America's Future, there is a difference between the work experience gained by students in a structured co-op program compared to that of students who work but not in school-supervised jobs. A study comparing co-op high school students and co-op students in two-year colleges with peers who had non-co-op jobs found:

Co-op students are more likely to:

- report that their jobs make use of what they learn in school
- report that what they learn on the job is useful in school
- see their current jobs as closely related to their careers
- report that their jobs provide abundant opportunities for learning
- feel their jobs to be intrinsically interesting and worthwhile

Controlling for grade level, gender, parents' education, reported GPA, and expectations for further education, co-op students they have:

- Greater use of reading and writing on the job
- greater use of other school-taught knowledge and skills
- more opportunities to learn new things
- greater interest and motivation to do the job
- greater use in school of what they learn at work

Co-oping Pays Off!

The advantage of co-op is not just an enriched academic education–

Benefits for the University

- Enriches classroom learning by student sharing of actual on-the-job experiences.
- Stimulates faculty and student research through relationships with cooperating organizations.
- Enhances learning, frequently providing students with access to "state of the art" equipment and technology.
- Provides more efficient use of campus facilities on a year-round basis.

Benefits for the Employer

- Co-op is an excellent source of interim and potentially permanent manpower.
- The infusion of bright young people, directly from an educational environment, provides new ideas and viewpoints that can be refreshing and stimulating.
- A co-op program can be developed to allow continuous job coverage so the employer does not have to be concerned about continuity.
- The program provides the company with a low-cost training mechanism. Co-op employees generally earn a salary below the average paid to new graduates.
- The co-op employee can be thoroughly grounded in established employer practices while still at a formative professional level.
- A co-op can free higher salaried professionals from some of their more routine tasks.

Benefits for the Student

- The integration of theory and practice provides greater meaning to classroom experiences and learning.
- The discipline-related work experience of co-op provides a smoother transition into post-graduation employment in a chosen career field.
- Students can obtain paraprofessional co-op positions in outstanding companies to which they might otherwise not have access.
- Co-oping contributes to personal maturity and enriches students' resourcefulness, self-confidence, self-discipline, and sense of responsibility.
- Co-op is an opportunity to earn significant income while learning in the workplace.
- Co-op experience enhances employment opportunities at graduation and beyond.
- Co-op offers opportunities to network with industry professionals and to develop mentor relationships with individuals who offer insights, advice, and encouragement.

The world does not pay for what a person knows.
But it pays for what a person does with what he knows.
—Laurence Lee

Co-op Outcomes Checklist

According to the National Commission for Cooperative Education, there are many outcomes from cooperative education. While education and practical learning are the fundamental outcomes from cooperative education, many of the by-products of the system benefit students, employers, and educational institutions.

Student Outcomes
- Able to integrate classroom theory with workplace practice
- Clarity about academic and career goals
- Motivated academically
- Technical knowledge gained through using state-of-the art equipment
- Understanding of workplace culture
- Workplace competencies and new skills
- Responsible work habits
- Career management and advancement skills
- Professional network
- Post-graduation employment opportunities

Employer Outcomes
- Access to well-prepared, short-time employees
- Flexibility with human resources assignments
- Cost-effective long-term recruitment tool
- Access to candidates with sought-after skills and backgrounds
- Increased staff diversity
- Partnerships with colleges and universities
- Input regarding the quality and relevance of curriculum
- Cost-effective productivity

Institutional Outcomes
- Recruitment of new students
- Retention of current students
- Wider range of learning opportunities for students
- More relevant curriculum
- Enhanced reputation in the employment community
- Improved rate of employment of graduates
- Increased alumni participation
- Linkage of college-to-business partnerships
- Increased support from corporations, foundations, and grants

Societal Outcomes
- Established model for workforce preparedness
- Income tax revenue produced
- Reduced demand for student loans
- More productive and responsible citizens
- Industry-education partnerships

CAUTION!

Be careful not to confuse some of the benefits of co-oping with the defining purpose of cooperative education. As described in this chapter, there are numerous professional, personal and financial rewards available to co-op students. But remember: cooperative education is designed to enrich a student's academic program with discipline-related, planned, monitored, and supervised practical experience.

Cooperative education complements–*but does not replace*–good college academic performance, financial aid, and on-campus work-study programs.

The primary purpose of education is not to teach you to earn your bread,
but to make every mouthful sweeter.

–James R. Angell

ACTIVITY ♦ ACTIVITY ♦ ACTIVITY ♦ ACTIVITY

Why Participate in Co-op

List five reasons, in order of importance, why you will be participating in the cooperative education program.

1. _____

2. _____

3. _____

4. _____

5. _____

What Do I Expect to Learn by Co-oping

List five personal learning objectives that you hope to achieve as a result of participation in the cooperative education program.

1. _____

2. _____

3. _____

4. _____

5. _____

♦ CASE STUDY ♦

Ethical Behavior within the Co-op Triad
Case One: The XYZ Company versus the ABC Company

    Margaret has officially accepted a co-op position with XYZ Company and has established her start date as January 1. She informed her co-op adviser and completed the necessary paperwork. However, in the last week of December, the ABC Company called to request an interview. Margaret went on the interview, was offered a position by the ABC Company, and accepted. On January 1, Margaret went to work for ABC. Her co-op adviser discovered this only when an XYZ Company representative called and asked where Margaret was, since she did not show up for work as prearranged. Answer the questions below using your school's co-op handbook or rules document (if available) as a guideline.

1. What do you think about Margaret's actions? Were they appropriate? Ethical? Professional?

2. What should the co-op adviser do about Margaret's actions?

3. If you were the XYZ Company, what would you do?

4. Should the ABC Company do anything?

♦ CASE STUDY ♦

Ethical Behavior within the Co-op Triad
Case Two: A Change in Assignment

Andy accepts a co-op position with Acme Products. The position seems perfectly suited to Andy's long-term career interests. But after two weeks on the job, the union goes on strike. All management (including co-op) personnel are expected to pitch in and do whatever is necessary. The department manager, Andy's supervisor with 25 years of experience takes responsibilities working on the assembly line. He asks Andy to help him on the line. Andy refuses, asserting that he doesn't have to do manual labor because that is not in his job description. Furthermore, he submits his resignation on the spot and walks off the job.

For Andy, the issue was not crossing a picket line–he was perfectly comfortable doing that. He just doesn't want to do the kind of work (that's not in his job description) required by the company's new situation. Answer the questions below using your school's co-op handbook or rules document (if available) as a guideline.

1. Did Andy behave like a professional? Explain.

2. Did the employer behave appropriately or inappropriately given the situation?

5. What role should the co-op adviser play in this situation?

4. What are the concerns and implications for Andy, the employer, and the co-op adviser?

♦ CASE STUDY ♦

Ethical Behavior within the Co-op Triad
Case Three: The All-female Office

A small insurance agency has one co-op position, described as a "general business" position. The co-op position is responsible for a wide variety of tasks depending on the daily needs of the insurance agency. All current office staff are women. Because the manager likes having an all-female office, she asks the co-op adviser to send her only female candidates. When the job list is distributed, some male students request that their credentials also be submitted to the insurance agency. The co-op adviser sends the resumes of both men and women students who indicated interest. The insurance agency office manager calls and angrily demands an explanation as to why she has received resumes from male students. Answer the questions below using your school's co-op handbook or rules document (if available) as a guideline.

1. Does the employer have the right to ask for only female students?

2. Should the adviser honor the employer's request and only send the female students that are interested?

3. Are the rights of male students being compromised? If so, how?

♦ CASE STUDY ♦

Ethical Behavior within the Co-op Triad
Case Four: The Non-enrolled Student

A mother calls asking the co-op adviser how her son can become involved in the co-op program. The mother states that her son is in his third year and is currently majoring in business. The adviser checks the student's records and discovers that the student has not been enrolled at the university for the past three quarters. It is obvious from their conversation that the mother thinks her son is still taking classes. To answer the mother's question, the adviser says, "I'm sorry but your son hasn't been in school for the past year. Since he's not a student, he can't co-op. Have him call me if he ever re-enrolls." Answer the questions below using your school's co-op handbook or rules document (if available) as a guideline.

1. Should the co-op adviser tell the mother that her son isn't taking classes?

2. Does a parent have the right to have access to this type of information?

3. What should the student do?

♦ CASE STUDY ♦

Ethical Behavior within the Co-op Triad
Case Five: Asleep on the Job

Answer the questions below using your school's co-op handbook or rules document (if available) as a guideline.

1/3/95	Larry begins his co-op employment with TWL Enterprises. After completing a thorough orientation, he is given four projects to work on.
1/16/95	Supervisor reported finding Larry asleep in his office. Another employee had found him sleeping earlier in the day. The Supervisor confronted Larry on this issue and reported it to the Area Supervisor. The Area Supervisor had received reports from several employees that Larry had been sleeping during work hours. This was again discussed with Larry along with concern that he might be ill or something. Larry denies having any trouble staying awake while at work or that there is anything wrong with him.
1/23/95	Larry does not show up for work. At 9:30 a.m., the Operations Secretary calls his apartment; Larry says he is sick. The Operations Secretary reminds him of the procedure for calling in if unable to be at work and refers Larry to the company doctor.
1/26/95	Larry is seen playing video games on the computer. His work was due but not completed. The Supervisor and Larry discuss not playing video games while at work and the importance of turning in work on time.
1/30/95	Larry sees the company doctor, who does some blood work. Larry falls asleep during a production meeting. Everyone in the meeting observes this.
2/3/95	Larry's projects are still not completed, and the Area Supervisor sees him leave the plant two hours early and pulled Larry's time records. The records indicated that Larry rarely spent 8 hours a day in the plant, although *each* time sheet he manually completed and submitted indicated that he did. Many days he took more than an hour for lunch. He was allowed 30 minutes. On one day, he worked only 5 1/2 hours.
2/4/95	Larry comes to work at 9:30 a.m. Results of the blood work indicate that Larry has no illness. Larry is fired and his co-op adviser notified.

Assume the orientation was thorough and covered all relevant company policies.

Which issues are ethical and which are more issues of professionalism on the job?

What could Larry have done to clean up his act?

How could Larry's behavior affect the company?

How could Larry's behavior affect the university?

What effect might the firing have on Larry's professional future?

CHAPTER 2

Learning through Cooperative Education

The highest activity a human being can attain is learning for understanding, because to understand is to be free.

–Baruch Spinoza

Co-op is a method of education that integrates applied experience with academic course work. While cooperative education may vary somewhat within different institutions, it should be a fundamental component of the academic curriculum. A good cooperative education program involves a progression of learning experiences that allow the student to gain a more complete understanding of knowledge already attained. The progressive learning experiences also build a foundation for future theoretical learning.

Integrated with theoretical instruction in a discipline area, the co-op assignment reinforces the corresponding learning objectives—objectives such as skill development in technical proficiencies, communication, business maturity, interpersonal ability, and decision-making. In many co-op work assignments, the level of responsibility on-the-job increases with experience and additional course work.

As symbolized by the co-op triad, your university and the employer are integral facilitators of your learning program. Your co-op faculty/adviser gives you guidance and supervises many aspects of your co-op program. Your employer designs co-op work assignments that are instructive and challenging; the employer also gives you feedback on your performance. But you–the student–are the primary and most active agent in your own learning. Learning through cooperative education, you will acquire new facts, skills, understandings, and attitudes. Co-op learning occurs, not just through a predetermined syllabus, but also through your individual experiences and your active involvement and reflection.

In a class, all students are taught the same material. That is, they read required chapters, do assigned projects and homework, and take tests over the same information. While on co-op assignment, there are also some common learning experiences. In addition to discipline-related technical knowledge, co-op students generally learn and enhance skills in analysis, decision-making, planning, communication, and interpersonal relations. However, each co-op student has a learning opportunity that is unique. Even two students who work at the same company are likely to learn different things. Why? Because as a co-op employee, a student has assignments and experiences–and learning opportunities–that will vary by the individual work setting. Daily work activities depend on other employees, customers, daily priorities, and other changing variables. In addition to this predictable variety, change is one of the defining characteristics in today's companies. Your co-op faculty/adviser and even your on-site job supervisor cannot foresee all the changes that might occur within a company, even during a single co-op period. The company may adopt new procedures, corporate directions, equipment, techniques, or management philosophies.

As a result, co-op students don't have a precise "syllabus" that determines all the experiences and learning opportunities they will encounter. This is one of the most exciting dynamics of learning through cooperative education. At the same time, you will have significant responsibility for shaping and focusing your own learning experience.

Learning at All Stages of the Co-op Experience

Learning through cooperative education begins well before your first work assignment. The first stage of learning through cooperative education occurs in the classes required in your academic discipline and major, both before and after a co-op work assignment. In many co-op programs, the next stage of learning is a formal course (such as this one) or a preparatory seminar that precedes the initial co-op assignment. The next stage of learning occurs as you and your co-op adviser conduct your search for a work assignment. The learning that occurs during the actual work assignment may be more visible than learning that occurs during other stages, but each stage offers important learning opportunities.

Stage I: Learning as a Student in the Campus Classroom

- How to transfer recent experience to classroom theory, activities, and case studies.

- How to process new classroom information within the context of your practical experience. Professors often explain the theory underlying the experiences you will have or have already had during your cooperative education assignment.

- How to ask the right questions to increase your understanding of the theory. As a co-op student, you will become accustomed to asking questions on the job to clarify your assigned duties. This skill will often carry over to the classroom.

- How to learn as a member of a team. Cooperative learning-where students study and learn as team members-has proven to be one of the most effective learning systems. Typically, your co-op assignment means working as part of a team, which will be useful for your academic work back in the classroom.

Stage II: Learning through the Co-op Job Search

- Tools and resources for assessing your skills, interests, values, and abilities.

- How to develop an effective resume.

- How to do company, field, and industry research.

- Various interviewing styles. Each interviewer is likely to conduct an interview a little differently. Which style do you prefer?

- Improved self-confidence through the interview process.

- An understanding of the needs of the workplace. Employers look for specifics that will meet their needs. What basic skills do most employers seek? Do you have them or, if not, how can you acquire them?

- Determine your current personal employment goals, realizing that they will likely change throughout the interview process and your entire career.

- Which positions that you interview for most closely meets your current needs and will fill the greatest number of both short-term and long-term goals.

- How to deal professionally with disappointment or rejection. (You may not be asked to interview by a company that you are very interested in, or, if you do interview, you may not be the candidate selected.)

- Standards of professional conduct, such as not continuing to interview after you have accepted a job, not waiting too long to respond to a job offer in the hopes of getting something better, and promptly notifying other employers when you have taken another offer.

- How to be positively assertive as you arrange and participate in interviews so that you have sound information for making a decision.

- How to make decisions and to take responsibility for your career path.

Stage III: Learning as a Co-op Employee

- The career field that you are planning to enter.

- Various industries that employ students with your background.

- Basic business etiquette and corporate protocol.

- Different corporate cultures. Companies have personalities just like people have personalities. The personality of the company is its culture.

- You may learn about office politics.

- You will learn about the career paths that others have followed. Every person that you speak with was your age once. How did they get where they are today?

In theory, any type of job will give you work experience, but this is different than learning. Without your active involvement and reflection, you might not be aware that learning is occurring, even in positions or situations where you are challenged.

Participating fully in an effective cooperative education program extends beyond merely attaining valuable work experience. Co-op is meant to be an essential part of a comprehensive education. Co-op students get valuable work experience while engaging in a systemized method of practical education.

The co-op advisers and on-the-job supervisors help students reflect, synthesize, and transfer learning between the classroom and the work environment. They also help students tap into *incidental* learning, learning that occurs in the background. Incidental learning may not become visible and lasting until the student, through discussions with a co-op adviser or supervisor, has the opportunity to apply, demonstrate, and articulate it.

Without active involvement and reflection on all dimensions of the co-op learning experience, a student might-wrongly-think, *"I didn't learn anything this co-op term"* or *"I didn't learn anything new."*

Action to be effective must be directed to clearly conceived ends.
–Jawaharal Nehru

Herman Schneider:
Intention Toward Student Learning

When Herman Schneider developed the cooperative education curriculum, he developed an educational initiative that has transcended time, disciplines, and programs. As a young civil engineering instructor, he noticed that students who best grasped the subject matter of his courses had practical experience. He believed that the fundamental theory taught to these men by the College could be complemented and, thus, would have more meaning to them if they could study the use of that theory in actual practice.

Even though students were exposed to machinery through pictures in a text or demonstrations in a lab, these pieces of machinery were merely abstract concepts. Once the student began to work with the machinery, it became more than a concept and its latent educational value was exposed. As the students began to work with a grinder or a lathe, for example, their minds would start to ask questions:

"Why is this machine designed this way?"

"Why do I need to add this lubricant?"

"What would happen if I added more or less?"

Complete answers to some of the students' questions might have to await further study. However, Schneider believed that the students' curiosity had been aroused by the practical experience. Schneider was certain that the practical experience had directed the students' thinking along educationally productive lines. He also observed that students' subsequent theoretical studies were noticeably more motivated and productive.

Schneider believed that, "Engineers, like doctors and lawyers, are trained for practice. Judgment based upon experience must supplement [classroom] theory."

On the following page, is the original co-op syllabus designed by Dean Herman Schneider, which illustrates the precise and comprehensive connections he envisioned through the integration of theory and practice–cooperative education.

Cooperative Education: One of the 10 Most Outstanding Engineering Education Achievements of the 20th Century

Cooperative Education is cited by the American Society for Engineering Education (ASEE) as one of the ten most outstanding Engineering Education and Engineering Technology Achievements of the twentieth century–an achievement that has had a lasting impact and has moved engineering forward most significantly. Other achievements in the Top Ten included the invention of the electronic computer, the development of distance learning, and the establishment of engineering standards.

–*Journal of Engineering Education,* January 1994

SYLLABUS OF THE COOPERATIVE SYSTEM
Original Syllabus of Herman Schneider, 1906

Objective	Method	Matter	Mechanism
TO PROVIDE ENGINEERING TRAINING FROM WHICH THE STUDENT SHALL ACQUIRE:			
1. A foundation in the basic principles of science.	1. Instruction in science and mathematics.	1. Chemistry, physics, mathematics, economics, practical engineering projects.	1. Class and laboratory work; coordination with practical experience.
2. Ability to use these principles in practice.	2. Gradual and natural advancement in practical work which uses these principles. Concurrent training in theory and practice.	2. An organized sequence in practical work. An organized sequence in science.	2. Cooperation with commercial concerns doing engineering work. Alternate periods spent by two groups of students at school and at practical work.
3. An understanding of engineering in general, as well as one of special department.	3. Varied exemplifications of theory in the classroom. Visits to a variety of engineering industries. Contact with different kinds of engineering.	3. Experiences of students in different types of work correlated with theory. Visits to waterworks, foundries, soap works, etc.	3. Illustrations furnished by coordinators and students. Organized shop visits.
4. A working knowledge of business forms and processes.	4. Instruction in economics, management, etc. Reports on shop visits. Analysis of show processes. Practical experience in business forms and procedure.	4. Fundamental principles of economics, systems, forms, contracts, patents in engineering work.	4. Coordination of classroom work with students' experience. Practical training organized by coordinators to insure experience in business forms and processes.
5. A knowledge of men as well as of matter.	5. Personal work with men from laborers up to superintendent or managers. Instruction in the basic elements of work.	5. Practical work, from laboring to directing. Fatigue, wage systems, employment, sanitation, etc.	5. Prearranged course of practical training.
6. Drill and experience in: a. Doing one's best naturally as a matter of course.	a. By regulating promotion work and pay on practical work. By maintaining a satisfactory standard in college work.	a. Practical performance; classroom performance.	a. Constant supervision and criticism of student's practical work. Consultations by college officials on advancing students on job. Internal coordination of college departments; conferences on student work.
b. Prompt and intelligent obedience to instructions.	b. By working under the rules of an industrial organization.	b. Practical work under foremen. Using practical experience in science courses. Work syllabi.	b. Student kept at manual labor until he learns to obey orders. Coordination of theory and practice. Study of syllabi.
c. Ability to command intelligently and with toleration.	c. By gradual rise to positions of responsibility in the cooperating companies.	c. Practical jobs of more and more authority and responsibility. Personal experience in hard work. Fatigue, wage systems, methods, sanitation, etc.	c. Success of student on practical and theoretical work checked by coordinators. Round table discussion in shop management courses.
d. Accuracy and system.	d. By practical work requiring mental and manual accuracy, and proceeds with a sequential orderliness. By insistence on accurate, orderly work.	d. Carefully selected jobs. Analyses of shop processes in class. All college courses.	d. Close familiarity with outside work through visits of coordinators. Coordination between departments to maintain standards.
e. Ability to write clearly and concisely, and to present technical matter interestingly before an audience.	e. By constantly requiring written work, and by requiring oral presentation of technical matter.	e. Reports on shopwork. Reports on shop visits. Laboratory reports. Engineering society papers and discussions. Class practice under criticism.	e. Coordination with English in criticizing all written work. Engineering societies afford practice in oral presentation. Exercises presenting reports.
7. An appreciation of humanity's best achievements.	7. Instruction in history and literature. Incidental instruction in art.	7. A general view of the development of civilization in both the useful and fine arts.	7. Class instruction and reading. Daily contact with art; optional courses in music, drawing, etc.
8. Ability to meet social requirements easily.			

Focusing Learning While on the Co-op Assignment

Supervisory Feedback

An important part of any cooperative education assignment is the feedback that you receive from your supervisor. Typically, feedback is given through an employee evaluation in which your supervisor assesses your strengths and weaknesses as they relate to your job performance. This feedback should be formalized through either a company or school performance evaluation form that is completed, discussed with you by the supervisor, and then submitted to your co-op faculty/adviser. Informal feedback in the form of compliments and constructive criticism is also extremely useful to you and your supervisor. These feedback processes are invaluable learning opportunities, and should be valued by both the supervisor and the co-op employee.

Improve your performance by improving your attitude.
–Life's Little Instruction Book

Remember: no one is perfect. All employees can improve upon their performance. When your employer points out areas for improvement, you should accept this feedback with the same vigor you would apply to improving your grades in a class. In this instance, the workplace is your classroom. Instead of trying to raise a grade to an "A", you will be trying to improve your performance to a superior rating or a specific skill to a higher level. Sometimes students are disappointed to receive "Average" or "Satisfactory" ratings thinking that they have done everything asked by the employer. However, on most performance evaluation forms, these ratings indicate that a student has met all conditions for completing an assignment—that is they have met deadlines, been accurate and productive. Normally this behavior is considered to be "Excellent" in the classroom and will earn you an "A." But doing "only what is required" in the workplace will only meet an employer's minimum performance standards. To earn an "Above Average" or "Excellent" evaluation, you will need to stand out from the other employees in some important ways.

A well thought-out employee evaluation can provide you with a tremendous amount of direction and enrich your education. Areas usually addressed in an employer evaluation are:

- Position Performance: quantity and quality of work, accuracy, ability to learn, technical knowledge, ability to transfer academic training to job, and ability to recognize and solve problems.

- Work Habits: organizational skills, willingness to take initiative, ability to cooperate in working relationships, ability to meet deadlines, attendance, and ability to work as part of a team.

- Personal Characteristics: professional maturity, motivation, self-reliance, leadership abilities, acceptance of constructive criticism, effectiveness in oral/written communications, and grooming.

Learning Agreements/Contracts

Learning is more rapid and efficient when you are a participant rather than a spectator. One way to participate in your co-op learning is by completing a learning agreement prior to a work term. A learning agreement lets you know what is expected on the job. It also lets your supervisor know your interests and what you need to learn. Supervisors can use a learning agreement to help motivate performance and measure success in meeting goals. You can use the learning agreement in a self-assessment of your progress, accomplishments, and growth. Learning agreements should be both qualitative and quantitative; they should address both student and employer objectives. They should also be flexible enough to be revised as circumstances require. Having a written report of objectives attempted and met during each co-op assignment can provide students, as well as co-op advisers, with a sequential profile of their professional progress.

Student Co-op Journals

Keeping a co-op journal allows students to participate and actively reflect on their own learning. Students evaluate their co-op experience and performance as it is taking place. Under this method, students periodically (usually weekly, sometimes daily) make journal entries of their current experiences and thereby capture them for future inspection. As you record materials, you will notice and reflect on various aspects of the work environment and task responsibilities. Your co-op adviser will read and discuss aspects of your learning experience with you.

Student Report

The student report is another method that facilitates students learning. Under this system, you would prepare a descriptive and evaluative report on your co-op assignment immediately following the work experience. Some schools provide a outline form that asks specific questions regarding the co-op experience just completed. Some schools require a written essay report that addresses specific topic areas. These reports are submitted to the co-op faculty/adviser for review and discussion.

Learning Modules

Another example of a multi-disciplinary academic assignment is the learning module developed by the University of Cincinnati. The learning module includes a Student Instruction Sheet, Student Project, Student Assessment Form, Employer Assessment Form and Faculty Assessment Form. It asks students from all disciplines to focus on the organizational culture of their co-op employer. Unlike some academic projects that require a paper on a topic area, this module asks pointed questions designed to focus the your learning on specific aspects of organizational culture. To complete this learning module, students ask their supervisors to help them identify an official statement relevant to the organization's culture such as a mission statement, a business or design philosophy, corporate goals or objectives, informational brochures or a personnel handbook. Throughout the term you will observe the day-to-day activities of the organization and compare the official statement on culture with what they observe. This becomes the basis for your project.

Prior to the end of the term, the student meets with the supervisor to discuss the student's new level of knowledge regarding organizational culture. The supervisor completes an Employer Assessment Form on Organizational Culture to provide an evaluation of the students' understanding on this topic. Students complete a form as well, assessing their own understanding of organizational culture. After the co-op term is completed, the faculty adviser will also evaluate the students' understanding of organizational culture. The objectives of this learning module include focusing students on specific learning pertaining to **Organization Culture** and to assess the students' learning from all three perspectives in the co-op triad. The University also utilizes learning modules that deal with **Proficiency in Technologies**, **Professional Ethics** and **Integrating Theory and Practice**.

Just as no two students are alike, no two supervisors are alike, no two co-op positions are alike, and no two co-op sessions are alike. Students will learn new things from each session of co-op that they complete. Each of the learning tools listed above will have their own strengths and detractions.

However, for any of these to be effective learning tools, they must be used within the context of a post-co-op instructional session with a co-op adviser. The co-op adviser will help you identify and process prior learning and prepare for how to incorporate it in your future learning, both in the classroom and in your next work assignment.

It is not ease but effort, not facility, but difficulty, that makes men.
There is, perhaps no station in life in which difficulties
have not to be encountered and overcome before any decided
measure of success can be achieved.
  –Samuel Smiles

Conditions for Effective Learning while on Co-op

Here are conditions that aid effective learning on the co-op assignment:

- Work that is meaningful.
- Environment that is congenial and compatible for the student.
- Student motivation to perform and to learn.
- Encouragement for students to take initiative.
- Student feeling that their work is important to the company.
- Relationship between co-op job and academic courses.
- Student input into decision making.
- Requirement that students relate job tasks to performance and goals.
- When students have a mentor or supervisor.
- Student knowledge of what is expected.
- Student awareness of the company and its products and goals.
- Student understanding of the purpose of job tasks.
- Student interest in the job and career area.
- Work tasks and skills that have direct, immediate application to the classroom.

We learn

10% of what we read

20% of what we hear

30% of what we see

50% of what we see and hear

70% of what we discuss

80% of what we experience, and

95% of what we teach

Cooperative Education Program
Job-related Learning Objectives

STUDENT   MAJOR   YR

A. By Student with Co-op Faculty/Adviser Initials   Date

OBJECTIVE	ACTIVITY
1.	
2.	
3.	
4.	

EMPLOYER   CO-OP SUPERVISOR

B. By Student with Co-op Supervisor Initials   Date

OBJECTIVE	ACTIVITY
1.	
2.	
3.	
4.	

NOTE: SECTION A must be brought to the quarterly interview with your Professional Practice faculty.

    SECTION B must be completed the first or second day of your co-op quarter with your co-op supervisor (see process).

LEARNING AGREEMENT

DIVISION OF PROFESSIONAL PRACTICE - UNIVERSITY OF CINCINNATI

STUDENT NAME CO-OP EMPLOYER (NAME & ADDRESS)

STUDENT MAJOR & GRADUATION YEAR

STUDENT WORK TITLE CO-OP SUPERVISOR'S NAME/TITLE

PROFESSIONAL PRACTICE FACULTY

JOB RELATED LEARNING OBJECTIVES (What I plan to learn)	ACTIVITIES (What I will do to accomplish the objective)	INTERFACE WITH COURSES (What courses were relevant to my objectives and/or activities)	EVALUATION (By Student)	EVALUATION (By Employer)
1.				
2.				
3.				
4.				

EVALUATION SCALE 0 = DID NOT MEET 1 = LIMITED ACCOMPLISHMENT 2 = ACCEPTABLE ACCOMPLISHMENT 3 = GOOD ACCOMPLISHMENT 4 = SUPERIOR ACCOMPLISHMENT

GENERAL COMMENTS

Project job-related learning objectives

Division of Professional Practice
Co-op Student Journal Report

PURPOSE

1. To help facilitate the highest level of learning while on your co-op assignment where you can test your abilities and practical applications to theory.

2. To help you begin to integrate theory learned in your classes with practical applications learned on your co-op assignment.

3. To help you in the career decision-making process.

4. This journal is for learning purposes only. It will become a permanent part of your cooperative education student file and will be available to faculty and administrators only.

While Cooperative Education plays a vital role in your professional development, it also serves as an important component of your overall learning in your academic discipline. After completing the co-op term, you should be more in tune to your interests and personal qualities. You should be able to better assess your values, decision-making skills and to understand the importance of setting goals. While learning more about yourself, you should also be able to point to specific concepts that you have learned in the classroom within your specific major or curriculum. For example, point to specific courses in your major and other requirements and electives in communications, computers, business, mathematics, psychology, etc., where you can see correlations in your academic and cooperative education.

GETTING STARTED

The first part of your journal should have the following:

A. Part A is applicable only to students who interviewed during the previous school term for a co-op assignment.

1. Please describe the referral and interview process that you experienced.

2. What did you learn when conducting your self-assessment and researching companies?

3. Did interviewers meet your expectations? Why or why not?

4. What type of questions did they ask?

5. What might you have done to better prepare for the process?

6. What is your general feeling about the job market?

7. What can your co-op faculty representative do to better prepare you for this process?

B. Complete the following information before (or shortly after) beginning your weekly journal entries.

1. Name.
2. Social Security Number.
3. Major(s).
4. Company name.
5. Name and title of supervisor.
6. Salary.
7. Describe the organizational structure. Where does your department fit in to the overall company?
8. What products or services does the organization sell?
9. What type of customers does the organization have–industrial, consumer, merchants, etc.?
10. What does your department do? What are your specific job duties?

WEEK ONE

Week one is usually set aside for orientation, training, and simply learning names and faces. During the rest of the term, pay close attention to the job responsibilities and tasks that are asked of you on a weekly basis in order to assess your own learning. Beginning with week two (you may start at week one if you desire), make an entry into your journal that addresses the following topics and other issues of interest to you.

WEEK TWO

1. Identify a short-term goal you would like to achieve while working at this firm. Has your supervisor shared expectations for your performance for the term? If possible, have your supervisor assist you in developing goals that will encourage your success. Try to arrange a short meeting (at your supervisor's earliest convenience) to discuss expectations.

2. If you worked in this position in previous co-op quarters and already have a good understanding of the duties, indicate in your journal how you can assume more responsibility and be more productive.

WEEK THREE OR FOUR

1. "Corporate Culture" is comprised of many different aspects of a corporate environment in which you work. Not always expressed in writing, a corporate culture can include such things as: acceptable clothing and grooming; expected number of work hours (especially for salaried professionals); preferred management style; employee behavior at work and outside; whom you lunch with; office formalities and structure; and age of

employees. During this week, observe the corporate culture and note items in your journal. Is this an environment that matches your own job values?

2. List some new procedures that you are being introduced to in your position (for example, computers, other equipment, or processes). If no new procedures have been introduced, discuss how you can make a larger contribution with your current knowledge or experience Rained in previous co-op procedures.

WEEK FIVE OR SIX

1. Have you received any formal (or informal) feedback on your performance? If so, what was discussed? What are you doing to enhance your performance? Things you might do to improve include: observing highly successful individuals in the department; reading company or equipment manuals; asking for advice. Are there company courses that may be at your disposal?

2. Is there anything you need to discuss with your supervisor regarding your performance? Indicate in your journal the outcome of your meeting.

WEEK SIX OR SEVEN

1. Showing that you are highly motivated and can take the initiative will be significant factor in your overall career success and add to your learning potential while on co-op. Describe how you have shown–or can show–initiative.

2. Describe an individual (no names) that exemplifies the type of professional you aspire to be or skills you desire to obtain. If no one in your immediate surroundings meets these criteria, describe an individual in another department.

3. Are there individuals that might serve as allies or formal or informal mentors?

WEEK EIGHT OR NINE

1. Identify the skills you have used in this position–for example, administrative, clerical, computer, writing, telephone, analytical, human relations.

2. How did you use these skills? How might these skills be useful in the future?

WEEK TEN

1. Did previous course work help prepare you for the responsibilities of this co-op position?

2. List courses that you plan to take when you return to school.

3. Will this co-op experience assist you in future classes? Why or why not?

FINAL ENTRIES

Entries are required for this section. There is no limit to the number of entries you can have in your final weeks.

1. Describe what you are doing and learning during these final weeks.

2. If you could change any aspect of this co-op position, what would it be?

3. Did the previous co-op session help you affirm your choice of major and determine your career goals?

4. What would you tell the next co-op employee to make his/her learning experience more beneficial?

LAST WEEK OF WORK

1. Describe a situation or accomplishment during the term about which you feel good. How did you succeed in this circumstance? Who benefited from your efforts–the company, the customer, a co-worker, your supervisor?

2. List the things or circumstances during this co-op session that you feel have been the most important to your overall learning experience. How will you use this knowledge in future co-op sessions? In the classroom? In your career?

3. On a scale of 1 to 4, with 4 equaling your highest level of learning from both positive and negative experiences, how would you rate the past co-op session? Explain your rating.

4. On a scale of 1 to 4, with 4 equaling your highest level of job satisfaction, how would you rate the past co-op session? Explain your rating.

YOUR COMMENTS

SECTION TWO

Components of the Co-op Job Search

The wind and the waves are always on the side of the ablest navigators.

–Edward Gibbon

CHAPTER 3

Career Planning

*The higher men climb the longer their working day. And any young man with a streak of idleness in him may better make up his mind at the beginning that mediocrity will be his lot.
Without immense, sustained effort he will not climb high.
And even though fortune or chance were to lift him high, he would not stay there.
For to keep at the top is harder almost than to get there. There are no office hours for leaders.*

–James Cardinal Gibbons

Participation in a co-op program gives students an excellent opportunity to begin a formalized process of career planning. Co-op students get a hands-on, pre-graduation preview of portions of their chosen career fields. In addition, co-op students have the opportunity to make important career decisions and plans on the basis of realistic expectations and reality-based experiences.

Career planning is a decision-making process that allows you to explore your career options. Consider the two words separately:

CAREER – something ongoing for which you train

PLANNING – the activity of creating a detailed guide for your actions

A good career plan provides you with definite goals that are realistic and attainable if you pursue them with effort and dedication. Your career plan at any given time is not intended to answer all the questions that emerge during your working lifetime. However, it can serve as a foundation and realistic guide for achieving personal satisfaction and job success.

The development of a sound *career plan* assumes that you have:

- Researched the professional opportunities available based on your individual strengths and interests
- Assessed your weaknesses and developed a program to alleviate or reduce them
- Completed an analysis of job options and their alternatives
- Learned the steps required to achieve specific career goals

For some students, planning is not an easy task. Some may fear making such important life decisions. Others may believe that "leaving all my options open" can take the place of career planning. However, if you plan your actions and research your real options, you have a much better chance of succeeding than if you passively wait for something to happen. Instead of career planning, some students rely solely on promises from personal contacts for career help–and may be disappointed. Personal contacts can be valuable resources, but they can't–or don't–always deliver for the job seeker. The best strategy is to rely on yourself, to plan, and to be prepared to take advantage of opportunities. Most of all, don't avoid this investment in your future success.

Career planning requires patience, persistence, and a systematic approach. Conducted as a step-by-step project, it will give you important information about yourself and your career options.

Don't be afraid to look at your faults.
—Yoruba Proverb

Step I - Self-Assessment

Self-Assessment is the initial, and perhaps the most important, step in the career planning process. Without successfully completing this first step, it is impossible to develop a sound career plan. Some individuals pay career consultants to do their career planning for them, but effective career planning is an ongoing do-it-yourself project. The self-assessment process in never completed because you continue to develop and grow–in interests, aptitudes, education, previous work experiences, likes, dislikes, strengths, and weaknesses. That's why everyone should periodically inventory their personal resources and ask, *"Who Am I?"*

Step II - Career Exploration

Career exploration requires you to answer the question, *"Who do I want to become?"* A thorough analysis of career options can provide you with alternative ways of achieving your most desired outcomes. It is impossible to review all existing careers but a starting point is to list areas of primary interest to you. Then simplify the list by eliminating career fields and positions that are incompatible with the information you gathered during Step I, your self-assessment.

Career exploration is the fact-finding stage where you use resources to gather information, review it, and formulate your decision factors.

Resources that can be used in your research include:

- The Internet – Using the World Wide Web has become one of the most effective and easy ways to find out about companies, industries and career field.
- The public library
- The campus career resource center
- *Million Dollar Director* (Dun & Bradstreet)
- *Standard and Poor's Register*
- *Thomas Register of Manufacturers*
- *Consultants and Consulting Organizations Directory*
- Industry and Trade Journals
- Chamber of Commerce information
- Annual Reports
- *Everybody's Business: An Almanac*

Researching Just to Stay Informed

No discipline or career field exists in a vacuum. They all interact and interrelate as pieces of the same puzzle the "global economy." Each discipline affects and is affected by changes happening as close as the neighborhood and as far as the other side of the world. As a young professional, you should develop the habit of staying up-to-date by listening, observing, and reading. Be aware of events in any arena-economic, social, political, at any level. Some countries as we knew them a few years ago no longer exist while new countries are emerging, some through painful processes. Change is happening rapidly and international needs are developing even faster. You must not only cope with change, but also be prepared to take advantage of them.

Routinely listen and watch the news, read all of the daily newspaper, and become familiar with national and international news magazines. Think critically about what you read. Ask yourself, "How is this event going to affect my career field or my company?" Bring these questions to your co-op supervisor, to your academic or co-op adviser, and talk about them with your peers. You will discover that events, changes, and priorities may influence your career choices and course selection. You may also find valuable information related to your co-op job or to a company in which you are interested.

The difference between the impossible and the possible lies in a person's determination.
– Tommy Lasorda

Information Interviews

Information interviews are different from job interviews. During a job interview, you are interviewing with a company that is evaluating you as a potential employee. During an information interview, *you* are conducting an interview to expand your awareness regarding your discipline. An information interview is an opportunity to talk with experts in your career field and to learn more about the variety of career choices and jobs for which you may qualify.

As a co-op student, you may be asked to conduct one or more information interviews using guidelines and a set of questions. Conduct practice interviews with your friends and family members to sharpen your communication (both listening and talking) skills. The more comfortable you are, the more you will be in control during the interview–and the more you will benefit from the information and discussion. You will find that an information interview is a chance to impress and demonstrate your abilities to the interviewee–a professional that may offer a future opportunity. There may not be a job opening now, but there might be one later or on the professional's network.

Information interviewing should not end with this assignment for your co-op preparation course. You should use information interviewing throughout your professional life–when you seek a career change or a move, or to build and expand your network. The style may vary with the purpose of your interview. For example, networking is usually casual and conversational. Whatever the specific need and situation, the primary goal of information interviewing is to help you explore your career field.

It is easier to go down a hill than up, but the view is from the top.
– Arnold Bennett

Step III - Decision Making

Decision-making is the end product of career planning. This is where you assimilate the information you have gained through the self-assessment and career exploration steps. In this stage of career planning, you determine goals and make decisions. Decisions made at this point do not guarantee success. They do mean that you are ready to put a plan in motion. Some students avoid this decision-making stage because they mistake it for the final step of career planning. Some fear making "big" decisions that affect them for a lifetime. Others avoid making a career decision because of perceived family traditions or obligations ("Everyone in my family is a doctor; therefore, I should become one, too").

Both internal and external factors may affect your ability and willingness to make a career decision. It is natural to feel ambivalent about making important life decisions. Everyone entering college experiences some uncertainty about choosing a major or career field. But remember: decisions you make now are not irreversible. Career planning is an ongoing process that includes several opportunities for you to modify your plan.

Step IV - Course of Action

Once you have made some initial decisions, you will need to plan a course of action using information from your self-assessment and career exploration. Your plan should include both short-term and long-term goals. Your statement of goals should indicate a timetable for accomplishment and how you plan to reach them. You may determine that you need specific courses, more training, extracurricular activities, or more organization and community interaction (to gain experience or for networking). Be sure to identify specific weaknesses or limitations that need to be reduced.

Remember: each reduction of a weakness is attainment of a short-term goal so give yourself credit. Your co-op adviser is an excellent resource to you in this stage of career planning.

Step V - Verification

Verification, the final stage in the career planning process, provides you with a realistic view of career choices. This is where you get an opportunity to try out your dreams for real. A co-op program is an excellent opportunity to verify your career interests and "test drive" your career plan.

Career Plan Modification

Career Plans must be flexible enough to permit modifications because career planning is a continuous process. As circumstances change, you will change and have to adapt your career plan accordingly. One of the most obvious reasons to modify your career plan is that you have grown-have acquired new insights about yourself, your interests, and your opportunities.

Some other common reasons that lead to modifying a career plan are:

- Course offerings and new educational opportunities
- Job changes, transfers, and promotions resulting in new responsibilities
- Professional Practice experience (co-op)
- Marriage, family responsibilities, and physical health
- Military obligations
- Economic conditions
- Significant changes in cultural and social norms of society
- New technologies, jobs, and the evolution of the profession

After career decisions are implemented, new behaviors are put into practice. If outcomes do not meet specifications, changes are inevitable. No one can predict that decisions made will be the right ones at any time beyond the moment they are made. Change is healthy, growth is progress.

There is something that is much more scarce,
something finer far, something rarer than ability.
It is the ability to recognize ability.
–Elbert Hubbard

ACTIVITY ♦ ACTIVITY ♦ ACTIVITY ♦ ACTIVITY

Identifying Transferable Skills and Abilities

Most students experience some anxiety about their first co-op job. These anxieties may be about their lack of academic preparation and actual job experience or general anxiety about their personal readiness to begin a professional experience like co-op. Learning how to identify the *transferable skills and abilities* that you have developed through your life experiences will give you confidence that you do have marketable professional skills and that you have used these skills in the past.

This exercise is designed to help you learn to evaluate your experience and then communicate the value of it clearly to others. This will build your confidence that you do, indeed, have something to offer to an employer, right now! The exercise will also help you prepare for the interview process.

These skills and abilities are called "transferable" because they are necessary to every thing that you do. You can "transfer" your abilities from one job to another and from one experience to another. While you may not be as technically capable or have as much job experience as someone else, you may have more developed skills and abilities in other areas. Being able to recognize and use your own skills and abilities will help you identify the skills and abilities of those around you. (For example, if you recognize that your supervisor has poor communication skills, rather than reacting to the lack, you can take positive action to help clarify what your supervisor expects.)

In-class Group Activity

Everyone has some event, incident, action, or activity that they consider an accomplishment. Sometimes other people recognize it as significant, and sometimes others don't realize how important it was to you and your personal growth. For example, some students consider being accepted to their first-choice university as a significant accomplishment; others may have never doubted that they would be accepted. Whatever your specific accomplishment, if it was important to you, it is an event that you may use to analyze when attempting to identify your skills and abilities.

Make a list of your significant events, incidents, actions, or activities. From the list, select **two** these experiences that you can briefly describe in writing. Be sure that you will be comfortable discussing your selections with others.

continued

Homework Assignment

Write about the two experiences you selected, using no more than one page for each. Consider the following questions as you are write:

1. Why have I determined this to be an accomplishment? Was it difficult? Was it something new that I had to learn? Did I have to push myself in new ways? What parts of the process of making this happen were the most significant for me?

2. Did it have meaning for others? How did my actions affect or influence others? Were others even aware of my accomplishment? Did it change how others view me or interact with me?

3. Did my own awareness, attitudes, or behaviors change as a result of the accomplishment? Did I learn something I didn't expect? Do I deal with people differently as a result? Do I do things differently now?

4. What skills and abilities did I use to achieve this accomplishment? (List as many as you can.) The skills you use most often will be the ones you are aware of first. Don't stop there. This exercise is about learning how to identify skills and abilities, so dig deep and really think about what you had to do, think and/or learn in order to make this accomplishment happen. Be specific. For example, don't just say you used "good communication skills". This is too general and doesn't really say what you did. Instead, say, "I was able to instruct a group of individuals of diverse ages in the proper techniques of basic sailing", or, "I was able to help identify a group goal and motivate the group to complete that goal." By being this specific you will be able to see that there are perhaps hidden skills that you did not realize you possessed. The last example above is not just a communication skill; it is a basic leadership skill.

Small Group Presentation and Discussion

Many students have difficulty identifying skills and abilities beyond the most general ones. Working in small groups, you will get and give feedback. Groups should include no more than six students. Someone should volunteer to read first. After each person reads his or her description, the group then discusses the skills and abilities that they think were used. Feel free to ask questions about the accomplishment to clarify the skills and abilities used. Group discussion will give you a greater understanding of what others consider important. Take notes so you can review what is said. This exercise is also an excellent validation of your transferable skills and abilities.

ACTIVITY ♦ ACTIVITY ♦ ACTIVITY ♦ ACTIVITY

Self-Assessment Activity: Abilities and Skills

Self-Assessment involves taking an honest look at your strengths and weaknesses. The primary value of self-assessment as a step in career planning is learning how to use your strengths and to minimize weaknesses. Combined with career information, an accurate and comprehensive self-assessment will prove very useful to your career planning.

ABILITIES AND SKILLS

A. What academic subjects do you enjoy the most? (Consider college and high school courses.)

B. What subjects do you like the least?

C. What academic subjects have you found most difficult?

D. In what areas do you have the greatest abilities and skills? List at least three below, but list as many as you believe you possess. Examples of abilities and skills: intelligence, creativity, mechanical ability, leadership skills, artistic talents, sales ability, communication skills, athletic ability, etc.

1. 2. 3.
4. 5. 6.
7. 8. 9.

Continued

E. What are the three most satisfying accomplishments in your life?

1._____

2._____

3._____

F. What abilities and/or skills were involved in these three most satisfying accomplishments noted in E above?

E1._____

E2._____

E3._____

ACTIVITY ♦ ACTIVITY ♦ ACTIVITY ♦ ACTIVITY

Self-Assessment Activity: Personal and Work Values

Your value system is important to making a career choice and to investigating specific positions within a career field. A good match between your values, position, and career will help insure a productive and enjoyable work life. (Remember: job and career *alone* may not give fulfillment in terms of your values. Your personal, family and leisure time may be a more important source of fulfillment in these areas.)

This section is designed to help you identify, rank, and relate your values to your career planning. It is divided into two areas–Work and Personal Values. These areas overlap, in the same way that your personal and work life may interact.

PERSONAL VALUES

Rate the values listed below. Place a check in the column which most accurately reflects your feelings. Carefully consider each decision when rating your values.

	Extremely Important	Very Important	Important	Somewhat Important	Unimportant
Close Friendship					
Community Involvement					
Financial Security					
Hobby/Hobbies					
Intellectual Stimulation					
Power or Status					
Honesty					
Marriage and Family					
Leisure Time					
Living Environment					
Freedom					
Travel					
Helping Society					
Helping Others					
Adventure					
Moral Fulfillment					
Other (Specify)					

ACTIVITY ♦ ACTIVITY ♦ ACTIVITY ♦ ACTIVITY

Self-Assessment Activity: Personal and Work Values

PERSONAL VALUES

Place a check in the appropriate category of the scale for each value listed. Use only *one* check per item.

Example:	Cold	___	___	___	X	___	Hot
High Pay		___	___	___	___	___	Average Pay
Eight-to-five Job		___	___	___	___	___	No Set Work Hours
Structure Setting		___	___	___	___	___	Unstructured Setting
Short Vacation		___	___	___	___	___	Long Vacation
Abstract Problems		___	___	___	___	___	Concrete Problems
Little Travel		___	___	___	___	___	Lot of Travel
Work Alone		___	___	___	___	___	Work with Others
Highly Competitive		___	___	___	___	___	Little Competition
Work Indoors		___	___	___	___	___	Work Outdoors
Less Variety		___	___	___	___	___	More Varied
Job Security		___	___	___	___	___	High Risk
Close Supervision		___	___	___	___	___	Little Supervision
Constant Deadlines		___	___	___	___	___	Few Deadlines
Problems Requiring Long Investigation		___	___	___	___	___	Problems with Quick Solutions
Leadership Role		___	___	___	___	___	No Leadership Role
Frequent Relocation		___	___	___	___	___	No Relocation
No Entertaining		___	___	___	___	___	Necessary to Entertain

Technical Problems	_____	_____	_____	_____	_____	People Problems
Urban Setting	_____	_____	_____	_____	_____	Rural Setting
Little Need for Manual Dexterity	_____	_____	_____	_____	_____	Need for Dexterity
Detailed Job Description	_____	_____	_____	_____	_____	Ambiguous Job Description
Work With People	_____	_____	_____	_____	_____	Work with Equipment
Work with Data	_____	_____	_____	_____	_____	Work With People
Scientific Impact	_____	_____	_____	_____	_____	Economic/Social Impact
Self-Initiative	_____	_____	_____	_____	_____	External Pressure
Desk Job	_____	_____	_____	_____	_____	Work Mobility
Other _____	_____	_____	_____	_____	_____	Other _____
Other _____	_____	_____	_____	_____	_____	Other _____

ACTIVITY ♦ ACTIVITY ♦ ACTIVITY ♦ ACTIVITY

Integration of Personal and Work Values

From the list of Work Values on the preceding pages, select your five **most important** (from either the left- or right-hand columns) and rank them in terms of their importance to you. List the most important value **first.** For example, if High Pay is the most important, list it first; if Work Outdoors is next in importance, list it second, etc.

1. _____
2. _____
3. _____
4. _____
5. _____

From the list of Personal Values on the previous page, select your five most important and rank them in terms of their importance to you. List the most important first, etc.

1. _____
2. _____
3. _____
4. _____
5. _____

Consider the PERSONAL and WORK VALUES you have just ranked. Select the top three values and rank order them.

1. _____
2. _____
3. _____

ACTIVITY ♦ ACTIVITY ♦ ACTIVITY ♦ ACTIVITY
Self-Assessment: Personal Understanding

A. What kind of person are you? What do you think of yourself as an individual? List below your strong points (determination, cheerfulness, intelligence, etc.) and your weak points (easily angered, impatient, impolite, etc.).

Strong Points
1. _____
2. _____
3. _____
4. _____
5. _____

Weak Points
1. _____
2. _____
3. _____
4. _____
5. _____

B. Are you satisfied with yourself? If not, what personality characteristic do you want to change?

_____
_____
_____

C. What old habits would you like to break?

_____
_____

D. Are there new habits you would like to develop?

_____
_____

E. Have you worked at improving yourself? If yes, how?

_____
_____

ACKTIVITY ♦ ACTIVITY ♦ ACTIVITY ♦ ACTIVITY

Self-Assessment: Leisure Time Activities

A. How much "free time" do you typically have in a week? That is, time <u>not</u> spent in classes or getting to classes, personal hygiene, eating meals, studying, working, or normal nighttime sleeping.

_____

_____

B. On the chart below, check how you spend your free time. Check as many as appropriate. Indicate total hours per week for the **three** activities that receive or require the greatest amounts of your leisure time.

Activity	YES	Total Hours/Wk for Top Three
TV Watching		
Socializing with friends on- or off-campus		
Organizations (campus, church, community)		
Participate in sports (games and practice)		
Attend sporting events as a spectator		
Reading		
Hobbies (models, sewing, collecting)		
Attend movies, concerts, theatre, etc.		
Hang out (with friends, at the mall, etc.)		
Telephone time with friends		
Family-based socializing		
Other (specify)		

continued

C. How do you feel about your leisure time? Too much? Not enough? Feel guilty about wasting time? Doing nothing? Discuss briefly.

_____
_____
_____
_____
_____
_____
_____

D. Are there new activities you would like to undertake in your spare time? If yes, list potential new interests not currently being pursued.

_____
_____
_____
_____
_____
_____
_____

ACTIVITY ♦ ACTIVITY ♦ ACTIVITY ♦ ACTIVITY

Self-Assessment: Time Management

One of the most important learned skills is how to use your time effectively.

Before we can truly manage our time, however, we need to look at how we currently are using the 168 hours in each week. When we take a close and honest look at how we currently use of time, it is possible to make decisions about re-allocation to provide additional hours for existing or new activities.

The following pages are charts divided into the 24 hours of a day. There are four columns for you to record your activities during each hour. Some hours may be devoted to only one activity (watching TV, for example). Other hours may include a combination of activities (studying and lunch, for example).

The chart on the next page is an Example Page already completed. The next three pages are for you to record how you spend your time for three weekdays. To be most helpful to learning more about your use of time, activities should be recorded as you proceed through the day.

For three weekdays, record what you do each hour or part of an hour. Use broad descriptions such as: attending class, working, sleeping, eating, telephone time, travel (driving or walking), watching TV, socializing, class preparation (studying, reading, library time, etc.), time alone (doing nothing in particular).

EXAMPLE ♦ EXAMPLE ♦ EXAMPLE ♦ EXAMPLE
Time Management - Sample Daily Record

Hour	Activity #1	Activity #2	Activity #3	Activity #4
Midnight-1 a.m.	Study	Personal time	Sleep	
1 - 2 a.m.	Sleep			
2 - 3 a.m.	Sleep			
3 - 4 a.m.	Sleep			
4 - 5 a.m.	Sleep			
5 - 6 a.m.	Sleep			
6 - 7 a.m.	Sleep			
7 - 8 a.m.	Personal time	Breakfast		
8 - 9 a.m.	Travel (auto)			
9 - 10 a.m.	Class			
10 - 11 a.m.	Class			
11 - Noon	Library			
Noon - 1 p.m.	Library	Lunch	Socialize	
1 - 2 p.m.	Class			
2 - 3 p.m.	Lab			
3 - 4 p.m.	Lab			
4 - 5 p.m.	Library	Study		
5 - 6 p.m.	Study	Travel (auto)		
6 - 7 p.m.	Dinner	Study		
7 - 8 p.m.	Study	Travel (auto)	Shopping	
8 - 9 p.m.	Shopping	Travel (auto)	TV	
9 - 10 p.m.	TV	Telephone	Snack	
10 - 11 p.m.	Study	Telephone		
11 - Midnight	Telephone	Personal Time	Sleep	

♦TIME MANAGEMENT CHART #1♦

Date_____   Name_____

Hour	Activity #1	Activity #2	Activity #3	Activity #4
Midnight-1 a.m.				
1 - 2 a.m.				
2 - 3 a.m.				
3 - 4 a.m.				
4 - 5 a.m.				
5 - 6 a.m.				
6 - 7 a.m.				
7 - 8 a.m.				
8 - 9 a.m.				
9 - 10 a.m.				
10 - 11 a.m.				
11 - Noon				
Noon - 1 p.m.				
1 - 2 p.m.				
2 - 3 p.m.				
3 - 4 p.m.				
4 - 5 p.m.				
5 - 6 p.m.				
6 - 7 p.m.				
7 - 8 p.m.				
8 - 9 p.m.				
9 - 10 p.m.				
10 - 11 p.m.				
11 - Midnight				

♦ TIME MANAGEMENT CHART #2 ♦

Date _____   Name_____

Hour	Activity #1	Activity #2	Activity #3	Activity #4
Midnight-1 a.m.				
1 – 2 a.m.				
2 - 3 a.m.				
3 - 4 a.m.				
4 - 5 a.m.				
5 - 6 a.m.				
6 - 7 a.m.				
7 - 8 a.m.				
8 - 9 a.m.				
9 - 10 a.m.				
10 - 11 a.m.				
11 - Noon				
Noon - 1 p.m.				
1 - 2 p.m.				
2 - 3 p.m.				
3 - 4 p.m.				
4 - 5 p.m.				
5 - 6 p.m.				
6 - 7 p.m.				
7 - 8 p.m.				
8 - 9 p.m.				
9 - 10 p.m.				
10 - 11 p.m.				
11 - Midnight				

♦ TIME MANAGEMENT CHART #3 ♦

Date _____   Name _____

Hour	Activity #1	Activity #2	Activity #3	Activity #4
Midnight-1 a.m.				
1 - 2 a.m.				
2 - 3 a.m.				
3 - 4 a.m.				
4 - 5 a.m.				
5 - 6 a.m.				
6 - 7 a.m.				
7 - 8 a.m.				
8 - 9 a.m.				
9 - 10 a.m.				
10 - 11 a.m.				
11 - Noon				
Noon - 1 p.m.				
1 - 2 p.m.				
2 - 3 p.m.				
3 - 4 p.m.				
4 - 5 p.m.				
5 - 6 p.m.				
6 - 7 p.m.				
7 - 8 p.m.				
8 - 9 p.m.				
9 - 10 p.m.				
10 - 11 p.m.				
11 - Midnight				

After you have analyzed how you have used your time for these three days, answer the following:

1. What three categories of activities require the most time?

   Activity   **Average hours per day**

   1._____   _____

   2._____   _____

   3._____   _____

2. Were you surprised by any of your feelings? That is, are you spending more or less time on certain activities than you realize?

   _____

   _____

   _____

3. What activities would you like to spend less time on?

   _____

   _____

   _____

4. If you had 10 more hours in the week, how would you use your "bonus"?

   _____

   _____

   _____

   _____

   _____

Pulling It All Together

You have now completed the Self-Assessment Assignment. For your own knowledge about *yourself,* review the total activity by asking yourself these questions:

- Is the person in the Self-Assessment really you?
- Do you know this person?
- Is the person you've described well suited for the college major you have selected?
- Is the person you've described well suited for the career field you have selected?
- How compatible are your personal and work values?
- Do you want or need to change how you use the 168 hours in each week?
- Are you satisfied with yourself?
- Are there self-improvement projects you can initiate?

ACTIVITY ♦ ACTIVITY ♦ ACTIVITY ♦ ACTIVITY

Career Analysis Activity

This exercise will help you gather and analyze career information. A specific job category or a career field will be explored through research of the available literature and, if possible, an interview with a professional in your selected position or career field.

The assignment is to write a 500-word (approximately) paper about your career field and, if you have one, a specific job choice. Some career field examples are: Accounting, Management, Personnel Administration, Marketing, Mechanical Engineering, and Graphic Design. Some specific job examples are: Public Accountant, Retail Store Manager, Director of Personnel, Marketing Research Analyst, Research and Design Engineer, Computer Graphics Artist.

Use a minimum of four publications for your research **OR** two publications and an interview with someone currently employed in the career field or specific job.

In the paper, devote a paragraph to each of the following:

1. A brief description of what the career field or position encompasses. (What do people do in this career field or position?)

2. The general qualifications required, including specialized skills or knowledge and or licensing requirements.

3. Employment outlook for this career or position over the next five to ten years.

4. Current starting salaries (average or range), and potential earnings after ten years or more. Include information about benefits, commissions, bonuses, etc.

5. On the basis of your research and interview, discuss the personal rewards (satisfaction) of this career field or position. Consider such things as compensation, enjoyment of work, status, working conditions, travel, etc.

6. List five major reasons for choosing this career field or position.

7. List the five factors that concern you the most about your career/position choice.

At the end of the paper, list all your research sources. For published material, include the title, author, date of publication, and page numbers. For interviews, include the name of the person you interviewed, job title, company, and date and length of the interview.

CHAPTER 4

Goal Setting

Nothing comes merely by thinking about it.

−John Wanamaker

Defining goals and objectives is a crucial part of developing a sound career plan. Goal development is a formal, ongoing, and time-consuming process that results in career guidance and direction. Goals can be defined as the end result or an achievement where an effort was directed. According to Rouillard (1993), goals become realistic when you can answer the question, "What's In It For Me?" (W.I.T.F.M.)

While individuals respond differently to different assigned projects, we all have a tendency to commit strongly to the achievement of goals whose outcome produce personal rewards. Goals can be dreams, thoughts, long-term or short-term, quarterly, annual, future, or an ultimate destination. Goals should be somewhat broad, but measurable. Objectives, on the other hand, clearly define specific steps needed to accomplish measurable goals. The more time you give to developing specific objectives, the more likely you are to get a positive outcome.

The goals and objectives you choose for your personal and professional life are not carved in stone. As you change through experience, your interests will change. What appears important today may not be important tomorrow. Sometimes you will encounter obstacles that impede or slow progress toward your goals and objectives. This may be time to revise your goals, objectives, or both. If you feel trapped in activities that are unproductive, reviewing or revising your goals and objectives may relieve the stress.

The process of developing goals, whether self-directed or a team effort, is designed to accomplish specific results. Things that happened in the past happened for a reason, whether or not you used a formal process to determine the path or direction you wanted to follow. If you have goals that motivate and energize you, success is not far behind.

Any person who selects a goal in life which can be fully achieved, has already defined his own limitations.
–Cavett Robert

Take a few moments and reflect on some of your past decisions.
- How did you get your first summer, part-time or full-time job?
- What were your plans after graduating from high school?
- What process did you use in selecting a college?
- Why did you decide to go to college?
- Why did you select a specific major?

Now reflect on the following:
- How much thought went into your responses?
- Were you in the right place at the right time?
- How involved were you in the decision-making process?

Your responses indicate the choices that have been made–or not made–that have led to where you are at this point in your life.

I have learned that success is to be measured not so much by the position that one has reached in life as by the obstacles which he has overcome while trying to succeed.
—Booker T. Washington

Elements Involved in Establishing Goals

Sukiennik (1984) identified four aspects of successful goal setting:

1. Determine sacrifices you are willing to make in order to satisfy personal and professional needs
2. Assign realistic time parameters to reach specific goals.
3. Set high goals that can be measured and attainable
4. Establish a reward system that is both internal (feeling of success) and external (something tangible).

Setting goals can be an uncomfortable experience. It requires you to focus on yourself, to take control of your own destiny, and to plot your next step. Your direct participation in setting your own goals involves: developing specific goals to be accomplished; projecting timeliness and outcomes; and identifying any sacrifices you need to make.

Scenario 1

Your goal is to earn "A" in all your basic fundamental courses. But achieving this goal requires a lot of time and effort. How would you accomplish this goal?

What are the issues?

What are the options?

Scenario 2

The sales department at XYZ Company is expanding its workforce. Each sales associate has been assigned a new territory and directed to increase their client pool by 20% by the end of the fiscal year. How can this be accomplished?

What are the challenges?

What steps need to be taken?

What is the projected outcome?

What is the expected timeline?

Scenario 3

You have two employment opportunities: (1) a promotion to a new position without a salary increase but with increased responsibilities and work that is directly related to professional goals; or (2) a position with a salary increase and valuable training, but no opportunity for future growth.

What are the issues?

What are the options?

Which is the best opportunity? Why?

After determining the risks involved and identifying appropriate action plans, put your goals on paper. The act of recording your goals and being able to look at them validates the process. Even at this stage, assign specific time parameters to each goal. By connecting a goal to when it can be achieved you connect goals to your reality.

Categories of Goals

For clarity, categorize your goals by the *type and level* of need that they meet.

Essential Goal

Necessary, ongoing, and recurring activity or improvement needed on a regular basis

Problem-Solving Goal

Elimination of a specific problem that needs attention or immediate action

Innovative Goal

Not problem-solving or essential, but desirable

Understanding these concepts will help you determine the appropriateness of your goals to your career and personal issues. Here are some examples of goals by category.

Essential	Declare a major at meeting with academic adviser on Thursday, 2:00 p.m. so that I can apply for major/degree candidacy.
Problem-Solving	Design a display that has eye catching appeal, promotes the product, stays within the assigned budget and can be completed by the end of the day.
Innovative	Develop database system that would allow equal access to users.

Writing Goal Statements the S.M.A.R.T. Way

Goal statements lay the groundwork for the achievement of specific goals. Goals are achieved as a result of implementing a plan, monitoring its progress, and revising objectives. If necessary, restart the cycle. Developing goal statements the S.M.A.R.T. way requires each statement to be:

Specific — The statement outlines in detail what is to be accomplished, so there are no misunderstandings. General and vague goals are irrelevant.

Measurable — The statement must be quantifiable in order to provide a standard for comparison. It is not enough to say that you want to change something and not give any indication as to how much.

Action-Oriented — The statement describes those activities that are action-oriented and needed in order to accomplish the goal.

Realistic — The statement must be practical and attainable when pursued with interest and motivation. Goals must relate to the accomplishment you wish to achieve in life.

Trackable — The statement must contain time parameters, must be observed and be cost effective. (Powell, 1990).

In short, **S.M.A.R.T.** goals demonstrate commitment.

ACTIVITY ♦ ACTIVITY ♦ ACTIVITY ♦ ACTIVITY

Goal Development Worksheet

Step One. Develop and list two to three goals for each category.

Essential Goals

_____
_____
_____
_____

Problem-solving Goals

_____
_____
_____
_____

Innovative Goals

_____
_____
_____
_____

Step Two. Choose and mark your highest priority goal from each category.

ACTIVITY ♦ ACTIVITY ♦ ACTIVITY ♦ ACTIVITY
Developing Goals the S.M.A.R.T. Way

Using one of the goals from the previous activity:

1. Describe a goal statement that is **Specific.**

2. Describe how the goal will be **Measured.**

3. Describe the **Action-Oriented** activities.

4. Describe how the goal is **Realistic**–practical and achievable.

5. Describe how the goal is **Trackable.**

ACTIVITY ♦ ACTIVITY ♦ ACTIVITY ♦ ACTIVITY

Goal Setting Action Plan

Using the material you developed in the two previous exercises, summarize the information in your Goal Setting Action Plan.

I. **Specific Goal** (write one goal)

(Example: To become a _____ in five years.)

II. **Measurable Objectives** (write two to three objectives)

(Example: To research the field of _____.)

III. **Action-Oriented Activity** (write two to three activities)

(Example: Visit college library and Career Resource Library to get information regarding the field of _____.)

IV. **Realistic**

(Example: Read College Bulletin to review requirements for the field of _____.)

V. **Trackable Evaluation**

(Example: All objectives will be successful if I decide to continue in field after __ years.)

CHAPTER 5

Guidelines for Resume Preparation

Excellence always sells.
—Earl Nightingale

What Is a Resume?

Your resume is the essential tool for obtaining a career-related co-op position. In essence, it is an autobiography of your personal, educational, and work history, condensed on a piece of 8 1/2 x 11 inch paper. An effective resume not only tells a potential employer who you are and what you have done through your experiences and skills, but it also demonstrates your ability to organize and present relevant information. While it is true that students can sometimes sell themselves in an interview, an effective resume is a powerful tool that can open the door to make that interview possible.

What Is the Purpose of a Resume?

A resume is a marketing tool. It is an advertisement of YOU. You are the product that must be sold. Your resume allows you to market your skills and experiences to a wide variety of prospective employers. To do this effectively, your resume must fulfill four main objectives:

Attract Attention

Your resume must introduce you and provide the information the employer needs to appraise and evaluate your qualifications for a position. But it should do so in a manner that attracts the recruiter's attention. One of the best ways to do this is to provide the recruiter with a resume that is highly "readable." That is, through a consistent pattern of organization and presentation, have you provided the reader with a way to easily scan your history and readily extract relevant information?

Create Interest

Your resume should open the door to an interview with the employer. Your resume serves as your direct-mail advertisement so make sure that you have written it to sell yourself. Emphasize your strengths and accomplishments while still providing a potential employer with the full picture of you as an individual.

Communicate Accomplishments and Skills

Tell the employer why you should be considered for a position. Use action verbs to describe your experiences. View your experiences from the standpoint of a potential employer. What did you gain that would be valuable to the organization? Your descriptions should stimulate further conversation in an interview.

Provoke Action

If the content and readability of your resume stands out in the crowd, it will usually lead to an interview. After the interview, your resume should serve as a reminder of who you are, what your past experiences are, and what assets you offer as an employee. In some instances, a co-op employer may skip the interview stage and hire solely on the basis of an effective, clear resume.

The harder you work the luckier you get.

–Gary Player

The Benefits of Preparing Your Own Resume

- ♦ The preparation process helps clarify your thinking about who you are and what you have done.

- ♦ When you prepare your resume, you also prepare yourself to be more effective in the interviewing process.

- ♦ Preparing your own resume on the computer allows you to store your organized information for long-term use. Keeping it on a diskette will give you easy access for corrections, adjustments, and additions needed in the future.

- ♦ Some employers ask applicants to completed resume forms available on the employers' websites. These resume applications should be filled out with the same meticulously. Employers will often scan them in search of specific skills, while evaluating your writing ability.

> *Though computerized resume wizards and templates can offer content and formatting assistance, they should not be substituted for your own creativity. In order to be effective, resumes require effort from you and should reflect your personality and style. Wizards and templates are generic tools that may not meet your specific needs. However, many will allow for formatting and content modifications that make the resume your own.*

Requirements for Preparing a Resume

There are many templates and software programs that can be used to develop your resume. These "canned" tools can make the process of resume development easier, but they are not a substitute for a thoughtful planning. When choosing a style and format, be careful to pick one that matches the amount and type of information your resume will include. Since it is an advertisement of you, your abilities and your accomplishments, it should also match your own personality. While matching your own personality, you also want to match the personality of the company or field you plan to enter. Preparing your resume cannot be effectively accomplished in one sitting. Rather it requires an evolving process of on-going experimenting, critiquing and fine-tuning on the part of you and others.

There are as many good resumes as there are personality types that develop them. Therefore, you will find a wide variety of opinions on what the perfect resume should resemble. Each human resources recruiter, co-op representative and career adviser will have a preference of style and format. However, there is little disagreement on what a poor resume looks like. The five "C"s below are guidelines for the how to prepare a good resume.

Clean

The first impression is very important so overall appearance must be attractive. Margins on all sides should be at least one inch. Use quality paper (preferably white, light ivory or light gray). Use a consistent layout and enough "white space" to avoid appearing cluttered or crowded. Use an easy-to-read style and size of type.

Concise

Use short forceful phrases—no sentences or personal pronouns (1, my). Use action verbs. Avoid unnecessary words and don't repeat phrases or information. The one-page resume is appreciated by most employers. Some employers may ignore a resume that goes beyond one page unless there is an obvious reason for the length.

The perfect advertisement is the one that makes people happy they bought what it was you were advertising.
—Anonymous

Correct

Be sure all information is accurate and your final version is error free. Edit it yourself and have someone else check it again. Employers assume that your resume is the best product you are capable of producing. If your best includes mistakes then you won't be a good employee for them.

Concrete

Be as specific as possible about your accomplishments.

For example, *Responsible for training 10 new employees over a two-year-period.*

Credit Yourself

Emphasize the "best of you" and how you would be an asset to the employer. Present yourself as a professional. Sell yourself in an orderly, reasonable manner. Be sure you can easily discuss your personal, educational, and work history when asked.

What Is the Order of Items in a Resume?

Heading

Include your full name. It is usually centered at top, but many computerized resume developers place it in other strategic locations. Immediately below, your college address on the left and your home (permanent) address on the right. If your home and campus address is the same, place the address under your name and eliminate the "Home Address" title. Include your current telephone number. (If an employer can't reach you easily, someone else will get the offer.) Students that have email addresses and homepage websites may choose to include them in the heading. Many employers use this form of communication. A word of caution on including homepages—Make sure your website sends the appropriate message about your professionalism, character and ability. Consider how employers will evaluate your homepage as well as its "links."

Job Objective (optional)

This is a brief description of the type of position you desire. If it is too general, it becomes irrelevant; if it is too specific, it can limit your opportunities. A job objective may not be required or necessary for some co-op positions. For a full-time position, the objective can be included in your cover letter. Including a job objective can be beneficial if it adds to your "sales pitch." The objective statement should tell a prospective employer what you can do for the company and should be tailored to the specific position to which you are applying. Do not use it to explain what you want in a job. Students with dual majors (or majors and minors) and those applying for a position outside their academic field can use a job objective to give direction to the resume. A job objective may also be useful when responding to a classified ad or a personal referral.

Education

In **reverse** chronological order (most recent first) list name of school, location, years attended, class, degree, and major(s). Include both college and high school. Academic honors may be included here or under "Experience" (see below).

Skills / Qualifications

List special skills acquired through formal or informal education, work, or life experiences. Be descriptive and be prepared to expand your description in an interview. (For example: *Fluent in written and spoken Spanish.*) List the operating systems and software you can work in (for example, DOS, WINDOWS, Macintosh, WORD, WordPerfect, Microsoft Office, AutoCAD, Lotus 123, PageMaker, Quark, Mathematica, Photoshop, SysStatSpreadsheets, etc.) If used strategically, this heading may replace the job objective in some circumstances.

Experience

In reverse chronological order, list the names and locations of the companies where you have worked. Indicate whether the positions were full-time, part-time, or summer employment. Describe your responsibilities with action verbs and emphasize your achievements. (See the list of action verbs toward the end of this chapter.) Positions can be paid or unpaid; describe unpaid positions as volunteer experience. Do not include the reason for leaving a job.

Achievements / Scholarships / Awards (optional)

Use this category only if you can list two or more items. If you have only one item, it can be listed in the education or experience section.

Activities

In reverse chronological order within each subhead, list activities separately under subheadings of college, high school, and civic or community.

Interests (optional)

Include specific hobbies, sports, musical instruments, etc. Be careful not to identify yourself by race, religion, political affiliation, etc.

Personal Data (optional)

Personal data (marital status, date of birth, health status) in general should not be included in a resume. Unless this information is directly related to the requirements of a position, employers should not request it and you should not include it. (An example of a possible exception would be a legal age requirement for a sales position.)

References

Include the statement "References available upon request." Do not list actual references on the resume, but have them readily available if they are requested by a prospective employer. In selecting your references, choose individuals who will give you positive, enthusiastic recommendations. And always ask someone's permission before giving a name as a reference.

Salary Objectives

Never include a desired salary on your resume. If you are asked about salary in an interview or on an application, answer that salary is "open" or "negotiable." Through your research of the company and career field, you should have an idea of the salary range available for the position you seek.

When someone wants to hire you, even if it's for a job you have little interest in, talk to them. Never close the door on an opportunity until you've had a chance to hear the offer in person.
–Life's Little Instruction Book

*A man's mind, once stretched by a new idea,
never regains its original dimensions.*
–Oliver Wendell Holmes

Resume Types

While there are many acceptable types of resumes, this section discusses the four types that are most frequently used. ***The chronological resume is most common and most appropriate for cooperative education experiences.***

Chronological Resume

This kind of resume lists experiences in reverse chronological order (most recent first). It is an "attendance record" that is a history of where you were at what point in time. Because your experiences are ordered by time, not their salability, the chronological resume may not market your qualifications to the specific position you seek. Because of the limitations of this type of resume, you must carefully describe your background to effectively illustrate your abilities and accomplishments.

Analytical Resume

This is the format most often used by individuals with little experience. It lists in order of importance the experiences that best market your job objective and demonstrates that you possess skills, abilities, and training.

Functional Resume

This type of resume highlights the specific job functions or job titles of your previous positions. It describes results in terms of achievements and emphasizes skills and talents. It places less importance on company names and dates. This resume is a very effective marketing tool when attempting to illustrate qualifications for a specific job.

Creative Resume

This kind of resume has "eye-catching" appeal. It is also the most difficult type to design. It can combine features from all other types of resumes. Individuals who use this format are attempting to stand out from all the rest. This approach is most successfully used by design and art applicants. It has also been successfully used by individuals who are attempting to re-enter the workplace after a long period of time. Since many recruiters tend to be conservative, this type should be used with caution.

A variety of sample resumes have been provided at the end of this chapter. Each has differences in format, style, design, and descriptions. As you review each resume, identify the features and styles that you prefer and that would best reflect your skills and experiences at this time. Also refer to the list of resume do's and don'ts for suggestions on preparation of an effective resume.

Resume Preparation

DO's and DON'Ts

DO

- Collect all necessary information to ensure that the content is accurate.
- Decide on the appropriate resume format (Chronological, Analytic, Functional, or Creative) and remain within this framework throughout the resume.
- Omit first person pronouns (I, me, my).
- Use short, forceful phrases (not sentences) that begin with active verbs in the past tense (directed, supervised, analyzed, conducted, developed, etc.).
- Make sure your spelling, punctuation, and grammar are perfect.
- Plan the layout. Make the resume long enough to read but short enough to sell.
- Allow adequate margins and white space between paragraphs for emphasis and neatness.
- Accentuate the positive.
- Emphasize accomplishments and focus on potential benefits to prospective employers.
- Prepare a rough draft. Get it all down on paper even if the final draft is a long way off.
- Edit and re-edit.
- Have someone critique the resume for errors and clarity of information.
- Double-check the final copy to be sure it is absolutely error-free.
- Be comfortable about the way the resume looks and reads.

DON'T

- Be pompous or wordy.
- Take ten lines to describe something when two lines are enough.
- Include anything negative.
- Minimize the importance of an experience by using qualifying adjectives such as *non-credit* courses or *unpaid* work.
- Mix formats within your resume (unless it is a Creative resume).
- Include geographic preferences or limitations unless absolutely necessary.
- Expound on your philosophy or personal values.
- Let someone else prepare your resume.

YOUR RESUME SHOULD

- Have instant eye-appeal, be attractive, and be easy to read. The initial visual impact of your resume is your "first impression" on a prospective employer.

- Be uncluttered and neatly blocked.

- Be organized so the reader will quickly zero in on the key points. (If you use more than one page, the most relevant information should be on the first page.)

- Be produced on standard 8 1/2 x 11 inch quality paper, preferably bond. (Odd-sized paper is difficult to file, mail, and duplicate.)

- Be a credit to your achievements, creativity, and ability to express yourself.

- Be professional and business-like.

- Promote your ability and potential, not just your experience and education.

- Focus on what you can do for the employer based on the evidence of your past accomplishments.

- Be tailored to the particular job or organization you are applying for.

- Be on one page. If two or more pages are used, be sure there is very good reason that will be obvious to the reader.

- Indicate that "References will be furnished upon request." Get permission before offering someone as a reference.

- Be prepared on a computer and printed on a high quality laser printer or ink jet printer.

YOUR RESUME SHOULD AVOID

- Unnecessary data. Include only essential information to emphasize it.

- Hard-to-read, fancy, too big or too little, and casual typefaces.

- Cover sheets, fancy folds, gimmicks, and unnecessary paper.

David W. Padur

Padurdw@his-emailadress.edu

College Address	**Permanent Address**
220 Campus View, Apt. 1	693 Close Knit Drive
Boston, MA 02167	Familyville, CO 01010
(617) 401-1111	(719) 001-9998

EDUCATION

9/97 - Present   Northeastern University, College of Arts and Sciences. Major - Economics, class of 2000.

9/94 - 6/96   Boston University, University College. Earned Associate's Degree in Liberal Arts.

9/90 - 6/94   Familyville High School, Familyville, Colorado. Graduated June 1994, college preparatory program.

WORK EXPERIENCE

9/97 - 3/98   Project Assistant for Wilmer, Cutler & Pickering, International Law Firm in Washington, D.C. Co-op responsibilities included assisting partners, associates, and legal assistants with researching, organizing, preparing and analyzing data; compiling data for a banking database; indexing documents; obtaining documents from government agencies; and other miscellaneous support tasks.

6/97 - 9/97   Full-time Machine Operator at Amko Plastics Inc. in Denver, CO. Summer work. Worked as a machine operator in the production of plastic bottles.

6/96 - 9/96   Full-time grounds and maintenance person for Shoreline Properties at the Plaza Hotel and Astor Hotel in Milwaukee, WI. Summer work. Did all landscaping and light repair work.

1/91 - 12/95   Engaged in variety of work during High School on full and part-time basis. Jobs held included: Dayton Daily Newspaper (Dayton, CO), Kettering Tennis Center (Kettering, CO), Dayton Country Club (Dayton, CO), Virginia Hollinger Memorial Tennis Club (Oakwood, CO), McDonalds (Dayton, CO).

COMPUTER EXPERIENCE

Experience in MS Office 97, WordPerfect for Windows, Spreadsheets, Databases, Corel Draw, and R:Base.

ACTIVITIES AND INTERESTS

Skiing, tennis, camping, traveling, music (playing guitar), tracking the stock market and other financial markets.

REFERENCES

References available upon request

LOIS KATHERINE ROBERTSON

Current Address	**Permanent Address**
2711 Delightful Drive	777 Lucky Lane
Cleveland, OH 44106	Smile, CA 99999
(216)209-7777	(411)777-1111
robloka@her_university.edu	

OBJECTIVE To obtain a co-op position with a company which will enable me to learn practical applications of the Political Science major while using my skills writing, customer relations, WordPerfect and LotusNotes.

EDUCATION

Bachelor of Arts, June 2001

Case Western Reserve University, Cleveland, OH
College of Arts and Sciences, Political Science
Grade Point: 3.0, Dean's List Spring 1998

Diploma, Northmont High School, June 1996

WORK EXPERIENCE

FIFTH THIRD BANK: Co-op December 1998 - March 1999
- Human Resources Department
- Utilized interviewing, business, and communications skills
- Performed daily functions of a corporate recruiter

Dayton Community Blood Center: Co-op July-September 1998
Also worked part-time July to December 1998
- Registrar - Donor Services Department
- Responsible for explaining different blood programs to donors
- Responsible for registering donors to give blood

United Appeal Telefund: April-June 1997
- Responsible for calling former contributors and asking for donations

M.J. Carroll: June-September 1996
- Sales Associate
- Aided customers in merchandise selection

ACTIVITIES

Kappa Alpha Theta Social Sorority
- 1998 - Derby Days Chairperson
- 1998 - Homecoming Chairperson
- 1997 - Assistant Rush Chairperson
- 1996 - Secretary of pledge class

Communication Association Seeking Excellence (C.A.S.E.)
- 1998 - Won 1st Place Trophy for Creative Writing
- 1996 to present - Secretary and head of Public Relations Committee

University Public Relations Officer
- Responsible for giving weekly campus tours for prospective students

REFERENCES Furnished on request.

LYNNE TAYLOR ································

LTAYLYN@UCMAIL.UC.EDU
http://www.ltaylyn/ucnet.com

College Address
1234 Career Path Blvd.
Cincinnati, OH 45220
(513) 000-9888

Permanent Address
198 Hiking Trails Rd.
Happy Glen, OH 45233
(019) 310-5437

Computer Skills

MS Excel	MS WORD	C++
Pascal	CorelDraw	UNIX

Education
University of Cincinnati, Cincinnati, OH. College of Business Administration.
Majors: Information Systems. BBA Degree expected June, 2001. GPA 3.5/4.0.

Work Experience
UC. Bookstores, University of Cincinnati, Cincinnati, OH. September 1997-April 1999.
Cashier. Responsible for opening and balancing cash registers, preparing 1997-1998 financial aid charges, taking inventory of texts, and handling sales transactions.

Lintegrity, Inc., Happy Glen, OH. June 1995-Sept. 1995 & June 1996-Sept. 1996.
Assistant. Responsible for the preparation of clients for the cosmetologist, preparing and serving refreshments, laundering linens, opening and closing, and sanitizing the salon. Promoted to Assistant from Receptionist.
Receptionist. Responsible for greeting clients, serving refreshments, answering phones, booking appointments, receiving/recording/pricing all inventories, dealing with suppliers, filing, retail sales, handling of all money, preparing the day's transactions for recording, balancing the register.

Activities
- VP of Parliament of Sawyer Hall 1999
- Kappa Alpha Theta Sorority
- Student Alumni Council
- President of residence hall floor
- Student Government, Political Action Committee

References
Available upon request.

Carlie N. Varga

Home Address
4153 Megan Drive
San Jose, CA 95125
(408)971-3243
varga@design.edu

College Address
432 Joker Road Apt. 5A
Riverside, OH 92521
(818)666-4627

Participating in the Professional Practice Program, alternating quarters of college study with work.

Education
University of California Riverside – Computer Graphics Major
Design Minor – Graduation 2000.

Marian High School, San Jose, CA
Graduated June 1995 – top 10% of class

Work Experience
Cincom Systems Inc.
3350 Ruther Ave. Cincinnati, OH
March - June 1999
Co-op design position with a computer software manufacturing company. Responsibilities include design of brochures, posters, conference materials, forms product fact sheets, and mechanicals, as well as contacting paper houses and collecting printer bids.

Bruce Design
11735 Chesterdale Rd. San Francisco, CA
March - June 1998 and September - December 1998
Worked in a co-op position for a multidisciplinary design firm. Responsibilities included assisting designers, copy setting, mechanicals, comps, logo design, illustration, and light designwork, such as letterheads and small brochures.

Mr. Dan Aemi, Forensic Engineer
4150 Pillars Dr. Los Angeles, CA
February - March 1998 and June - August 1998
Performed freelance illustration of automobile engine for publication with accompanying article and designed a small brochure to advertise changes in the company.

The Little Tikes Company
2180 Barlow Rd. Hudson, OH
March - June 1997 and September - December 1997
Worked as a co-op student in the design department of a large toy manufacturing company. Responsibilities included mechanicals, layout, comps, stat camera, type setting, small design projects and assisting and observing at photo shoots.

Awards and Activities
Certificate of Merit - Art Director's Club of Cincinnati
Annual Show 1998

College - Dean's List eight quarters, University Admissions with Distinction Award

High School - Honor Roll and Dean's List four years; Selections 98 Art Show; Showing - Student Clay Invitational; National Honor Society; National Art Honor Society; Peer Ministry; School Paper, International Thespian Society President and Secretary, Drama Group - Student Director and State Manager

References and Portfolio
Available upon request

STEPHANIE SMITH

College Address
71408 Peach Place
Atlanta, GA 30332
(404) 123-4567

Permanent Address
8844 Voils Street
Lexington, KY 40503
(606) 765-4321

stephanie_smith@ga-robo/tech.edu

Work Experience

1998 - Present
Georgia Institute of Technology, Atlanta, Georgia.
Title: Robotic Research Assistant under E. Hall, Ph.D.
Design, modify, construct and maintain mobile robots.

1997 - 1998
CAE Associates, Macon, Georgia.
Title: Project Intern
Built and analyzed computer models of automotive components.

1995 - 1997
Other miscellaneous jobs included refereeing girls' softball games and delivering newspapers.

Education

1997 - Present
Georgia Institute of Technology, Atlanta, Georgia.
College of Engineering. Major: Electrical Engineering.
G.P.A.:   3.6/4.0. Class of 2002.

1994 - 1997
Tates Creek High School, Lexington, Kentucky.
G.P.A.: 3.85/4.0. Class rank: 15/269.

Activities

College
Robotics International - Vice President, intramural softball and volleyball.

High School
Varsity softball - Captain, Computer Club - President, Mathematics Club, Yearbook Committee, German Club, intramural volleyball and tennis.

Special Knowledge
Basic, FORTRAN, AutoCAD version 11 and 12, PASCAL, and C++. Strong mathematics background. Electronics background in designing, building, and testing circuits. Speak fluent German.

Awards & Scholarships

College
University Honors Scholarship, William A. Blees Scholarship, 2nd place at the Annual International Unmanned Ground Robotics Competition, Dean's List every quarter.

High School
District TEAM's competition - 1st place in 1997. Four superior ratings at State Science Day competition (1994, 1995, 1996 and 1997), National Honor Society, 1997 "Best In Math" award, Who's Who Among American High School Students. Honorable Mention All-State in softball.

References
Available upon request.

ADAM VINCENT WILLIAMS

vince@engrtech/scc.edu

COLLEGE ADDRESS
10234 Crooked Lane
Dayton, OH 45402
513/123-4567

PERMANENT ADDRESS
Route 1, Box D
Kettering, OH 45425
513/102-0000

EDUCATION

    1998 to Present
    Sinclair Community College, Dayton, OH
    Major: Engineering Technology. Class of 2000.

    1995 to 1998
    Mason High School, Mason, OH

EXPERIENCE

    Summer and Part-time, 1997 to 1998
    Peter Scales, Inc., Mason, OH
    Initial responsibilities included cleaning and painting. Was promoted to Service Assistant. Repaired and serviced scales. Supervised three people and, while the owner was on vacation, managed the entire operation.

    Part-time Spring and Fall, 1996
    Earl D. Jones Farm, Mason, OH
    Plowed, planted, and harvested crops. Performed all maintenance work on farm equipment.

ACTIVITIES

    College: Intramural golf and softball. Serve on the Student Tribunal Curriculum Committee.

    High School: Varsity golf and softball teams. Vice President of both the Student Senate and the Spanish Club.

PERSONAL BACKGROUND

    Early childhood spent working on grandfather's farm. Learned to use and repair a variety of farm and other equipment. The money obtained from work was used for college tuition and to pursue an interest in numismatics. Speak fluent Spanish. Enjoy traveling. Have spent two months in Mexico as part of the International Students Program.

REFERENCES

    Will furnish upon request.

CIARA D. FORD

fodrcd@purdue.chem-engstu.edu
77 Missouri Trail ♦ Kansas City, KS 70013 ♦ 111/222-3333

EDUCATION
Purdue University, West Lafayette, Indiana.
College of Engineering, September, 1997 to present. Major: Chemical Engineering. Class of 2002.

Northwest High School, Kansas City, Kansas.
Graduated in June, 1997. Received the Principal's Award for outstanding community service.

SPECIAL SKILLS
AutoCAD 13, DOS, WINDOWS, MS Word (for Windows and Dos), and FORTRAN.

EXPERIENCE
Full-time Summer, 1997.
L.W. Trent Construction, Inc., Kansas City, Missouri.
Involved in surveying, construction, and maintenance of county roadways. Proposed major change in maintenance techniques which is projected to save the company $60,000 per year.

Part-time, 1996 to 1997.
Driscoe Landscaping, Prairie View, Kansas.
Organized complete landscaping service employing six helpers. Mowed grass, trimmed shrubbery, and performed general yard care for both residential homes and commercial institutions.

Part-time, 1995.
Value City Department Store, Kansas City, Kansas.
Cashier and Customer Service Representative. Sold, stocked and maintained merchandise. Assisted customers with problems and maintained or developed positive customer relations for the store. Trained new employees.

ACTIVITIES AND INTERESTS

College:	American Institute of Chemical Engineers, Society of Women Engineers, Purdue Marching Band (brass section), Residence Hall Representative.
High School:	President of the Band Club and Section Leader in the marching band. Saltwater aquarium hobbyist.
Community:	Assistant Scout Master, member of community task force to renovate the city's recreation facilities.

REFERENCES
Will forward upon request.

The Purpose and Format of a Cover Letter

In many co-op programs, the co-op adviser refers student resumes to prospective employers and a cover letter is not required for your resume. However, with this exception, each time you send someone your resume it should be accompanied by a customized cover letter. Since it may not be possible to gear a resume to an individual employer, the cover letter allows you to introduce yourself and speak to a specific employer about a specific position.

Your cover letter should use the standard business letter format.

- The opening paragraph states why you are writing, identifies the position or type of work you are seeking, and explains how you heard about the opening.

- In the middle paragraph (or paragraphs), sell yourself. Tell why you want to work for this specific employer in this specific position or type of work. Summarize past experiences, achievements, and qualifications that make you the ideal candidate for THIS job.

- The closing paragraph refers to the resume you are enclosing and requests an interview. Give your telephone number and indicate when you will follow up this letter. In your closing sentence, thank the individual or company for considering your candidacy and that you are looking forward to hearing from them soon.

SAMPLE COVER LETTER

123 Fourth Street
Cincinnati, Ohio 45296

September 17, 1994

Ms. Lynneafta Taylor
Vice President, MIS Department
Discovery Technologies, Inc.
38942 South Michigan Avenue
Chicago, Illinois 60699

Dear Ms. Taylor:

I am replying to your ad that was featured on the co-op bulletin board at the University of Cincinnati. The co-op systems position you advertised sounds very interesting and matches my credentials.

While in the process of completing my Bachelor of Science degree with a major in computer science, I have been employed part-time with Computer Haven. For the past two years I have worked as an Account Clerk Assistant handling inside sales of high-tech equipment. Through my education and employment, I have developed the technical, professional and personal skills that you have listed in your classified advertisement. Some of my skills and accomplishments include: knowledge of PC's, UNIX, C, Assembler, COBOL, Lotus 1-2-3 and databases; excellent communications skills (both verbal and written); customer/user support abilities; a strong mathematical background with a problem solving aptitude, and the ability to work individually as well as in a team environment.

I am scheduled to begin my first co-op position in December. My resume has been enclosed for your consideration. I am available to travel to Chicago at most times; however, I will be in your area during the week of November 23. If you have no objections, I will contact you to discuss the match between my background and the systems position to be filled. I can be reached at (113) 987-6543.

Sincerely,

Ciara D. Rhodes

Enclosures

ACTIVITY ♦ ACTIVITY ♦ ACTIVITY ♦ ACTIVITY

Resume Peer Review Form

Instructions

1. Carefully examine your own resume to make sure that you have met the standards established in each criteria area listed below.
2. Exchange resumes with the person next to you.
3. Check the person's resume you are holding using the system below.
4. Return the resume to its owner.
5. Resume owners, exchange with the person on the other side who will also rank each item using the above scale.
6. Return resumes to their owners.

In the blank next to each category, rank the item using the following criteria:

E=excellent   G=good   F=fair   P=poor

Resume Checklist

Writer	Reviewer 1	Reviewer 2	Criteria
_____	_____	_____	Overall appearance creates a good first impression: type is easy to read, white space is adequate, spacing is consistent.
_____	_____	_____	There are NO misspelled words or typos.
_____	_____	_____	The contact information is complete: full name, address, and phone number (two if applicable).
_____	_____	_____	No use of pronouns (I, we, you, etc.).
_____	_____	_____	Education is in reverse chronological order and includes high school and college school names, locations, dates, class, degree, and major.
_____	_____	_____	Experiences are in reverse chronological order and include employer names, cities, states, dates of employment, and whether it was part-time, fulltime, summer, etc.

_____   _____   _____   Experiences are described using action verbs and in a way that emphasizes achievements.

_____   _____   _____   Achievements/Scholarships/Awards section is included (if appropriate). Items are easy to understand.

_____   _____   _____   Activities/Interests section (if appropriate) is included and is divided into subheadings for college, high school, and civic/community.

_____   _____   _____   Special Skills section (if appropriate) includes marketable skills that don't show up elsewhere on the resume (AutoCAD, programming languages, foreign language, drafting, technical writing, etc.).

_____   _____   _____   The resume ends with a statement to the effect that "References will be forwarded upon request", space permitting.

_____   _____   _____   Format is consistent within each entry, from entry to entry, and from section to section.

_____   _____   _____   The length of the resume seems appropriate. Preferably it is kept to one page. If it goes to a maximum of two pages, this seems justified.

_____   _____   _____   Based on this resume, the assumptions made about this individual are all positive.

_____   _____   _____   The resume presents information presented in the most effective manner possible.

For any areas that you ranked as fair or poor, please provide the resume writer with constructive feedback.

COMMENTS:

Action Verbs

This list of action verbs should be used as a resource in developing the experience, achievements and activities sections of your resume. However, they should only be used where appropriate. Do not distort or misrepresent the duties described. The verbs are divided into five sections for easy reference. Choose those that fit your duties most accurately.

PLANNED

devised	developed	examined	discovered	evaluated
designed	organized	investigated	appraised	estimated
planned	analyzed	studied	measured	solved
created	produced	originated	interpreted	determined

DIRECTED

operated	managed	guided	supervised	governed
commanded	controlled	regulated	directed	prescribed
designated	coordinated	adapted	eliminated	transferred
maintained	awarded	authorized	vetoed	removed

EXECUTED

motivated	encouraged	utilized	employed	administered
approved	observed	demonstrated	disclosed	published
notified	produced	created	built	formulated
increased	expanded	extended	augmented	supplemented
condensed	curtailed	reduced	minimized	converted
exchanged	replaced	conceived	authored	strengthened
activated	unified	combined	merged	consolidated
updated	modernized	altered	modified	transformed
balanced	established	stabilized	discontinued	assembled
computed	estimated	inventoried	surpassed	simplified
grouped	distributed	classified	terminated	initiated
introduced	economized	obtained	procured	collected
assumed	attached	exchanged	invested	sponsored
expedited	attained	executed	achieved	dispatched

SERVICED

disclosed	informed	communicated	taught	instructed
educated	guided	informed	trained	lectured
endorsed	guaranteed	accommodated	aided	assisted

ADVISED

conferred	consulted	publicized	notified	advised
reported	advertised	informed	demonstrated	displayed
exhibited	illustrated	advocated	counseled	instructed
acquainted	recommended	suggested	familiarized	

ACTIVITY ♦ ACTIVITY ♦ ACTIVITY ♦ ACTIVITY
Definition of Resume Terms

Part I

1. A resume is:

2. The purpose of the resume is:

3. The personal benefits of developing a resume are:

4. A resume must do four things:
   1. _____
   2. _____
   3. _____
   4. _____

Part II

There are four basic types of resumes that are most frequently used. In the spaces below, fill in the blanks with the appropriate responses.

5. _____
   Can be a combination of any and/or all types of resumes. Usually it is the presentation that is unique. Since being unique is important in today's market, this type of resume most effectively matches the "eye-catching" criteria and has been successfully used especially by design and art applicants.

6. _____
   States each experience in order of its occurrence regardless of its salability. List past employment by dates, in order with the most recent experience listed first. Essentially it is an attendance record. Note the most effective method of illustrating achievements or how a person could be of benefit to a prospective employer.

7. _____

States, in descending order of importance, those experiences that best sell you for your job objective. It is designed to show that you possess skills, abilities, and training to handle the job you seek, even if you have no paid experience to your credit.

8. _____

Describes results and achievements in terms of functions. You can highlight items when aiming toward a specific job target. Some examples of functions or areas of experience are: leadership, research/development, quality control, administrative services such as accounting and purchasing, production, maintenance, supervision and control systems.

♦ CASE STUDY ♦

Selecting Candidates to Interview Based on Their Resumes

You are a **RECRUITER** for a company with a small co-op program. Your company manufactures axles used primarily in the production of light-bed trucks. You serve as outsourcing for most of the large automotive manufacturers in the U.S. and in several Latin American countries. Historically, you have used your cooperative education program as the primary recruiting tool for hiring entry-level engineering graduates. As a result, you look at each co-op student as a potential lifetime employee that could lead your company to future greatness. Your training program will prepare each co-op for a career within your organization by rotating the student through several major departments in each of their available co-op terms.

At present, you are looking for a metallurgical or materials engineering co-op student. This student's initial assignment would be in the Materials Science Center for Technology. This assignment would consist of participating in failure analysis, vendor quality audit, and plant processing problem resolution. Specific involvement would consist of a wide variety of laboratory functions, including metallographic sample preparation and interpretation, hardness testing, tensile testing, scanning electron microscope examination, and sample heat treatment.

Question 1

Based on the description of the company and initial co-op assignment, what qualities will you, the RECRUITER, be looking for in a candidate?

Question 2

Based on the resumes on the following pages, which 3 candidates would you choose to bring in for an initial interview? Why?

Question 3

For each of the three candidates that you plan to interview, give examples of the questions that you might ask. Would you ask each candidate the same questions, or vary the questions based on each candidate's resume?

> **RESUME #1 FOR CASE STUDY**

JASON R. BURKE

burger@mate.uc.edu

College Address
2645 Dorothy Court
Cincinnati, Ohio 45219
513-571-9997

Permanent Address
1514 Judson Drive
Findlay, Ohio 45842
419-402-9008

EDUCATION

University of Cincinnati, Cincinnati, Ohio.
    College of Engineering, September, 1998 to present.
    Major: Materials Engineering. Class of 2003.

Findlay High School, Findlay, Ohio.
    Graduated June, 1998. Top 10% in a class of 450.

EXPERIENCE

Wilson Construction, Findlay, Ohio.
    June 1998 to September 1998.
    Painting, poured concrete, small construction and general maintenance duties.

Findlay Chrysler Inc., Findlay, Ohio.
    June 1996 to September 1997.
    Floater. In charge of all filing. Also employed as a cashier and receptionist. Improved money handling and customer relations skills. Summer and part-time.

AWARDS AND HONORS

Monica Barry Scholarship.
National Honor Society 1997-1998.
Outstanding Students of America 1997-1998.
Academic Awards (GPA 3.75 or higher) 1995-1998.
First Team All Buckeye Central Conference (Golf) 1996-1997.

ACTIVITIES/INTERESTS

Member of Sigma Alpha Epsilon Social Fraternity, Fall 1998.
Member of Executive Board in Fraternity.
Involved in many extensive philanthropic projects for fraternity.
Participated in golf, tennis, and volleyball intramurals and leagues.
Volunteer for the American Red Cross and YMCA.

> **RESUME #2 FOR CASE STUDY**

Henry M. Moran
moranhm2345@email.uc.edu
Maplewood Drive
Cincinnati, Ohio 45242
(513) 755-8923

Education
University of Cincinnati, Cincinnati, Ohio.
College of Engineering, September 1998 to present.
Major: Materials Engineering. Class of 2003. GPA: 4.0 out of 4.0.

Oak Hills High School, Cincinnati, Ohio.
Graduated in June 1998.
Grade Point Average: 4.0 out of 4.0.
Ranked 1 in a class of 528.

Experience
Summers of 1996 and 1997.
Loutec, Inc., Loveland, Ohio.
Laborer. General duties included punch press operation, diamond wire cutting saw assembly, and shop maintenance.

Summer of 1995.
Kings Island, Kings Island, Ohio.
Ecologist. Responsible for the clean, quality appearance of the park. General duties included park and restroom maintenance and customer service.

Scholarships and Awards
College of Engineering Dean's Honor List
Alpha Lambda Delta Society - the National Honor Society for college freshman
National Merit Scholarship
Ohio Academic Scholarship
Engineering College Freshman Scholarship
Oak Hills P.T.A. Scholarship
Mary Rowe Moore Admission with Distinction Award
Valedictorian - Oak Hills High School, class of 1998
1993 Presidential Academic Fitness Award
Who's Who Among American High School Students - 1998
Academic Achievement Award - grades 10, 11 and 12
National Honor Society - 1997 and 1998
Placed 15th in 1997 Ohio Test of Scholastic Achievement – Algebra II test

Activities
College: Student Member of the American Society of Metals (ASM), Student Member of the Minerals, Meals & Materials Society (TMS), and Alpha Lambda Delta Society.

High School: National Honor Society, German Club.

Personal Background
Born August 3, 1980 in Cincinnati, Ohio. Hobbies include numismatics, art and geography. Enjoy traveling. Have toured a total of 43 states, Mexico and Canada. Have visited a large number of American Revolutionary War battlefields. Consider hard work and academics essential for a good life.

RESUME #3 FOR CASE STUDY

MARTY TAYLOR

COLLEGE ADDRESS
2653 Bellevue Avenue
Cincinnati, Ohio 45219
(513)000-8349
marty_bellevue@hotmail.com

PERMANENT ADDRESS
5623 LaPlant Road
Marion, Ohio 43303
(614)000-9961
taylorfamily5623@aol.com

EDUCATION

1998-Present	University of Cincinnati, Cincinnati, Ohio. College of Engineering. Pursuing a B.S. Degree in Materials Engineering. Class of 2003.
1995-1998	Elgin High School, Marion, Ohio. GPA 3.2/4.0.

EXPERIENCE

1998-Summer 1997-Summer	Marion Dresser, Marion, Ohio. Worked in an engineering firm that designed large mining shovels and draglines. Responsible for revising blueprints of products due to engineering changes, as well as creating mechanical drawings of detail parts.
1996-1997	Hardee's, Marion, Ohio. General duties included customer service, running register, preparing food, and clean-up.

ACTIVITIES

College	Member of Beta Theta Pi Fraternity. Intramural Sports: Football, Softball, Tennis.
High School	Honor Roll, Varsity Tennis Team, Intramural Sports.

SKILLS & INTERESTS

Mechanical Drawing, Tennis, Art, Various Sports.

REFERENCES

Available upon request.

RESUME #4 FOR CASE STUDY

Charles M. Windford
15679 St. Augustine Drive
Cincinnati, Ohio 45099
(513) 930-8043
windridge@augustine.edu

EDUCATION

1998 - Present   University of Cincinnati, Cincinnati, Ohio.
College of Engineering. Pursuing a B.S. Degree in Materials Engineering, class of 2003.

1995 - 1998   St. Xavier High School, Cincinnati, Ohio.
Achieved second honors seven out of eight semesters.

WORK EXPERIENCE

1998 - Present   Gilbert Garage and Radiator Shop, Cincinnati, Ohio.
General maintenance on garage and mechanical work on automobiles. Responsible for parts inventory and control.

1996 - Present   Windridge Acres, Cincinnati, Ohio.
Summer work at a horse farm. General animal and facility maintenance.

1995- Present   Windford Oats and Grains, Lebanon, Ohio.
Quarter partner in family owned grain- farming business. Responsible for general maintenance and repair on the farm machinery.

1995 - 1997   Mariah's Restaurant, Cincinnati, Ohio.
Busperson, Dishwasher Manager, and Cook.

1993- 1995   The Iron Skillet Restaurant, Cincinnati, Ohio.
Cook, Busperson, and Dishwasher.

ACTIVITIES

Stage Crew coordinator and Light Crew member for Theater Xavier at St. Xavier High School. Responsible for the design and construction of stage, props, and light placement.

INTERESTS

Demolition Derby Racing and Four Wheel Flat Drag Racing, remote control airplanes and boats, automobiles.

RESUME #5 FOR CASE STUDY

Scott T. Miller

College Address
3987 Sinbad Avenue
Cincinnati, Ohio 45229
(513) 759-3945
scott.T@beammeup.uc.edu

Permanent Address
3219 Apple Tree Lane
Miamisburg, Ohio 45343
(513) 866-7922

Education
University of Cincinnati, Cincinnati, Ohio.
College of Engineering, September 1998 to present.
Major: Materials Engineering. Class of 2003. G.P.A.: 3.795/4.0.

Miamisburg High School, Miamisburg, Ohio.
Graduated June 1998. G.P.A.: 4.135/4.000. Class rank 6/270.

Work Experience
Summers of 1997 and 1998, Full-time.
Employed by Brian Witherman.
Painted interiors and exteriors of homes. Gathered proper painting materials and instruments for each painting site.

Summers of 1994 and 1995, Part-time.
Drug Emporium, West Carrollton, Ohio.
Stocked shelves and condensed stock room. Trusted with responsibility of handling money as cash register operator, clean-up, and store closing preparation.

1993 and 1994.
Miamisburg and West Carrollton News, Miamisburg, Ohio.
Distributed newspapers and collected money monthly.

Scholarships and Awards
College of Engineering Dean's List, The Mary Rowe Moore Admission with Distinction Award, Ohio Board of Regents Scholarship, Mound Elementary School Scholarship, National Honor Society, Who's Who Among American High School Students, National Junior Honor Society, High School Top Ten.

Activities
College: Alpha Lambda Delta Freshman Honorary, Sigma Nu Social Fraternity.
High School: Varsity gymnastics four years - Captain one year, Science Olympiad team, Ohio Achievement tests in Geometry, Biology, Chemistry, and Physics.

References
Will be forwarded upon request.

CHAPTER 6

The Portfolio

*There's no one else like you in the world.
Look what you can create!*

—Judith Jamison

What Is It and Why Will I Use It?

The literal definition of a portfolio is a portable case for keeping and protecting, usually without folding, loose papers and prints. In the arts and design fields, the word has a more specific definition–a portfolio is visible evidence and accountability of your work. Think of it this way. In the performing arts, a job applicant auditions for a part. For a candidate for an art or design position, the portfolio serves as an audition display of talent and accomplishments. In addition to verbalizing their skills and attributes through the resume and interviews, visually oriented design students have the advantage of illustrating their skills through a portfolio.

A portfolio should display what you know and have learned as well as the level of your capabilities. It can also indicate specific interests and abilities and reflect your personality and individual talents. Your portfolio presents tangible evidence of your qualities to an employer. As much as the resume (and perhaps more), your portfolio may be a critical element in determining whether or not you are offered a position.

What Makes a Good Portfolio?

There are some guidelines for preparing a successful portfolio, but they can be very subjective. The varying opinions concerning portfolios can be confusing, but there are three basic elements of a successful portfolio:

- Quality
- Organization
- Presentation

After you research specific information and collect opinions of those you value on the "how and what" of portfolios, the ultimate decisions are up to you. Always keep in mind that your portfolio is a reflection of you and your ability. Like the resume, your portfolio is a marketing tool. The work in your portfolio is part of the product you are trying to sell.

The nature and quality of your work will vary over time, progressing from your early efforts through graduation and beyond. You should include only your best work in your portfolio–it should not be a scrapbook of everything you've ever done. Decide which pieces to include in your portfolio by evaluating their consistency and quality. Then decide how to organize and present your collection of work. Good organization adds clarity and understanding to the material that you are presenting.

In essence, developing a successful portfolio is a design problem. Approach the task as you would any design challenge. Keep in mind the fundamental principles of good design–**form, space, line, color, texture, balance, continuity.** Use the same thought processes you would use to design a brochure (or product or garment) to design your portfolio. The only difference between these other design problems and the design of your portfolio is that you and your talent is the information being communicated and the product being sold.

The "problem statement" for developing your portfolio is: design a personal presentation that effectively showcases your abilities and capabilities within your career field. The effectiveness of your presentation will be determined by whether your talents and capabilities are immediately evident and easily evaluated in terms of the required qualifications and criteria for the position you're seeking.

When I walk into a room I assume I have to prove myself.
I know that...But I also know that I can prove myself.
−Yvonne Braithwaite Burke

When Will I Use My Portfolio?

If you're seeking a position in a design field, your portfolio will be used as part of an "in-person" interview process or mailed to a prospective employer who is evaluating your credentials. Your portfolio gives you the advantage of being able to present tangible evidence of the qualifications and credentials that you describe in your resume. When asked about abilities and proficiencies in an interview, you will be able to show evidence of them. Remember, however, your portfolio is not the only factor in determining who should be offered a position. The interviewer is hiring a person, not a portfolio. It is important to follow all the guidelines for a successful interview, using your portfolio to supplement your verbal communication skills with proof of your visual communication expertise.

When geographic location makes an in-person impossible, you will need to present your credentials in a "mail-away" portfolio. Since you don't want to send the originals, you must reproduce them, using the medium that most accurately represents them. Size, compactness, consistency, ease of evaluation, accurate descriptions of the work−all should be considered in preparing an effective "mail-away" 99 portfolio. The possible media include 35mm slides, photostats, computer generated proofs, Xeroxes, videotapes, digitized works on computer disks, and other electronic media.

Which Medium Is Best for a Portfolio?

The preferred medium for a portfolio used in a personal interview is your original work. Original work most strongly conveys your attention to detail, your command of your field, and your impeccable neatness. The physical portfolio that you use as part of an in-person interview can include a variety of media such as slides, photographic prints, printed pieces, blueprints, Xerox prints, computer generated prints, manageable 3-D models, and electronic media. If you use 35mm slides as part of your presentation media, have them in a slide tray and determine prior to the interview that a projector will be available. If you use computerized materials, determine which hardware and software the employer prefers. You may well have to prepare different versions of computerized materials to ensure that your portfolio can be viewed easily and accurately. (Remember, your sophistication in computer generated materials will be evaluated as well as the examples of your design work.)

Great works are performed not by strength
but by perseverance.
−Dr. Samuel Johnson

Format: What Type of Portfolio Case Should I Use?

The format for presenting two-dimensional pieces of artwork will depend on the type and style of portfolio case you choose. You have several options, including a zippered carrying case, a zippered case with ring binder and acetate sleeves, and a hardside attaché case. The zippered case with acetate or vinyl sleeves will automatically determine your format–your portfolio becomes a "book" of your work. If you use a plain zipper case or the hard-side case, all work should be mounted on pieces of illustration board that are approximately the same size.

Always consider the ease of presentation when choosing your portfolio format for "in-person" interviews. The size of the portfolio case should accommodate the largest piece of physical work that you want to present. Sizes vary from 8 1/2 x 11 inches to 24 x 32 inches and larger. Make sure the case is not too large–you need to be able to carry it easily. Also, consider the weight of the completed portfolio: fifteen to twenty pieces of illustration board mounted with your work -- plus the case -- can add up to a heavy load that is difficult to carry. A portfolio should be portable!

"Mail-away" portfolios can have numerous, individualized formats. While the mail-away portfolio is usually comprised of 35mm slides, it can also use one or more of the media suggested for physical portfolios. (For example, slides can be presented on acetate slide pages protected in a ring binder.) If you decide to design and construct your own mail-away format, keep in mind that the portfolio design should enhance your work and that it will also be assessed for design quality. If the portfolio design dominates or distracts from your work, it fails to present your credentials in the best light. A mail-away portfolio must identify and explain the projects and the solutions that make up your portfolio. To expedite the return of your portfolio, be sure to furnish a self-addressed, stamped envelope or mailer.

Contents: What Should a Portfolio Include?

The contents of your portfolio should convey your best abilities and range of skills. Student portfolios usually contain fifteen to twenty pieces. Your portfolio might include representative examples from foundation studies, photography, drawing, drafting, rendering, fashion illustration, croquis, typography, computer studies, model building, and studio projects. You may want to include additional work to illustrate other abilities and interests, for example, work from electives such as figure drawing, painting, or sculpture. Your portfolio can also include work from high school, freelance opportunities and, of course, from your co-op assignments.

In addition to showing finished work, your portfolio should demonstrate your design process. Many employers like to see at least one project from start to finish. A sequential presentation of research, thumbnail sketches, and rough ideas that led to your final design illustrates your thought process as a designer to a prospective employer.

The content of your portfolio should always be evolving. Throughout your education and your design career, your abilities as a designer should be progressing and improving. To accurately reflect your progress and growth, your portfolio must also continue to develop. You should regularly update your portfolio, replacing older, similar problems, with more recent (and usually more involved and advanced) design solutions. As a student, you should update your portfolios at the end of each school term and work term.

He who stops being better, stops being good.

–Oliver Cromwell

Sequence: What Work Comes First?

There should be a rationale for the sequence of material in your portfolio. You may use a chronological order, beginning with high school or foundation studies and proceeding to current work. Or you may organize your work according to subject: drawing, drafting, perspectives, photography, computer skills, rendering, model skills, etc. Choose the sequence that most effectively showcases your work and that you are most comfortable presenting.

Presentation: What Should I Say about My Work?

How you present the work in your portfolio is extremely important, because it indicates the rationale for your selections. The body of work was chosen for its quality. It is quality work not only because you earned an "A" for the work, but also because it fulfilled the objectives of the project. You successfully met the design challenge. You should communicate what you learned through the design process. This shows a prospective employer that you have a true understanding of what you are learning.

Be sure to give enough background for each piece so that interviewers can accurately evaluate the contents of your portfolio. Be as explicit and concise as possible. Projects that are self-explanatory are just that ... don't over explain. Remember, this is your opportunity to express yourself concerning your ability. Make good use of it.

Learn to write well and you will be heard.

–Molefi Kete Asante

Putting together a portfolio is an extremely time-consuming task. Allow plenty of time for gathering your material, developing an appropriate format, and putting the presentation together. The successful portfolio cannot be designed and produced in a weekend or even in a week.

The Non-Design Related Portfolio

The portfolio can be an integral part of the job search process in non-design related professions as well. While the opportunities to use a portfolio effectively may be limited for co-op job searches, you may want to begin gathering information now for a portfolio to be used in a post-graduation job searches. A professional, business-like non-design portfolio can give you a competitive edge in the job market.

The visual aspect of a non-design related portfolio can include your resume, transcripts, letters of recommendation, performance reviews from past jobs, non-confidential reports you have prepared, publications that you have worked on, articles by or about you, certificates, recognitions, and diplomas you have received, and computer formats you have developed. Include all documents that highlight your previous performance, accomplishments, and abilities. Your portfolio should include a table of contents and be clearly organized. Effective types of organization include sections of specific skills or events, as well as chronological order.

The non-visual aspect of a non-design related portfolio is verbal. Whereas a design portfolio can physically demonstrate skills, you will need to verbally present your abilities. Decide what you want to convey (self-motivation, team player, initiative, communication skills, confidence, completing tasks, reliability, integrity, etc.) and then develop the written component of your portfolio around these topics. Your writing must be picture perfect. Ask someone to proofread your materials and ask your co-op adviser to critique the overall effectiveness of the portfolio.

Your written descriptions should be **specific yet brief.** Summarize activities and events. There is no need to include detailed explanations if you have included documentation in your portfolio. Use specific incidents to verbally illustrate your skills. Examples like the following can be very effective:

1. Explain how you were able to make quick, appropriate decisions to resolve a crisis during a babysitting job. Document the incident with a thank you note or letter of recommendation from the parent(s).

2. Describe how you progressed from an entry level position in retail sales, to lead sales, to a supervisory role, and then to being assistant store manager with responsibility for opening and closing. In your portfolio, include documents that highlight your meritorious performance in each role and your promotions.

3. Illustrate your performance on a prior co-op position. Describe a particularly difficult challenge that you faced and overcame. As documentation, include any awards, certificates, and write-ups in the company newsletter.

4. Describe leadership roles you held during high school and college in sports, groups, residence halls, or for special projects. Cite specific evidence of leadership such as resourcefulness, new programs, increased membership, and program impact.

Remember, the portfolio will be a reflection of you. It will represent your writing and communication abilities, as well as, your achievements, skills and recognitions. A good portfolio with distinguish you from the other applicants.

Note: You should have a few copies of your portfolio in order to leave one behind with employers if needed. Never give away your original documents.

The most important challenge in my life is to always test the limits of my abilities, do the best job I can at the time while remaining true to myself.
  –Mae C. Jamison

CHAPTER 7

Interviewing

No question is so difficult to answer as that to which the answer is obvious.
—George Bernard Shaw

Co-op students obtain co-op positions in one of three ways. Companies review credentials (resumes, portfolios) and:

1. Conduct personal interviews with candidates prior to making job offers.

2. Conduct telephone interviews with candidates prior to making job offers (this often happens when the position is located in a different city).

3. Hire candidates "sight unseen" with no interviews.

Most co-op students obtain positions as a result of being interviewed. But even students who are hired "sight unseen" for their co-op positions usually have participated in either an in-person or telephone interview.

How important is the interview for you? It is critical. **Most recruiters feel that they can assess a candidate's qualifications through an interview better than through any other means.** If you interview well, the employer may hire you. If you interview poorly, it is unlikely you will be hired. This is one side of the role of the interview in the employment decision-making process. There is, however, another, equally important side.

You have a decision to make. When you obtain a co-op position, you want a job that will give you learning experiences relevant to your career field and academic program. Co-op job experiences should help you develop the skills and abilities that will get you where you want to go professionally. You also want a job that will be enjoyable. How do you find out if a prospective co-op job is the position you're looking for? **The interview is your opportunity to learn about the job and to get the information you need to make an informed decision about the position.** Your questions you need to answer are: "Is this job best for me?" and "Do I want this position?" If you receive more than one job offer and can choose among employers, your answers to these two questions become even more important.

Remember, two important decisions occur as a result of each interview. The recruiter has a decision to make: "Should my company employ this co-op?" And you have a decision to make: "Do I want to work for this employer in this position?" Both the interviewer and the interviewee should be active participants in the interview, because both have very important decisions to make.

Interview Goals

Recruiters have three general goals that must be met through the employment interview:

1. Obtain relevant information about the interviewee. (This information will be used to decide whether the candidate is a good potential employee for the organization.)

2. Communicate relevant information about the organization and the job. (This will help "sell" the firm and job to the prospective employee.)

3. Make a tentative decision. (At the end of the interview, the recruiter must be able to decide tentatively if the candidate would be a good employee. As the interviewer talks with additional candidates, a candidate who initially appeared good might move down (or up) the scale.)

The job candidate also has three goals, similar to the recruiter's goals:

1. Communicate relevant information about himself or herself. (This information markets or sells the candidate to the interviewer.)

2. Obtain relevant information about the organization and the job. (The information will be used to assess whether there is a good match between what the job offers and what the candidate is seeking.)

3. Make a tentative decision. (By the end of the interview, the candidate must be able to decide tentatively if the position is a good opportunity. After interviews for other positions, this decision may be revised.)

The following chart compares the goals of the interviewer and interviewee. Notice that the goals are parallel. The recruiter wants to get information about the candidate and the candidate wants to communicate that information. This match between the two sets of goals helps determine how you can prepare for an interview.

Goals for the Interview

INTERVIEWER	INTERVIEWEE
1) Obtain relevant information about the interviewee.	1) Communicate relevant information about self.
2) Communicate relevant information about the organization and position.	2) Obtain relevant information about the organization and the position.
3) Make a tentative decision.	3) Make a tentative decision.

Preparing for the Interview

Preparation is key to a successful interview. As a job candidate, you must prepare to communicate relevant information as well as to obtain it. To prepare effectively and then interview successfully, you must:

- Know about yourself
- Know about the employer and the job.
- Do mock interviews.

Know Yourself

You are the expert in the employment interview. The recruiter wants to know about you, and you know more about yourself than anyone else does. **But even an expert needs to prepare.** When the recruiter asks about something you haven't thought about recently, you may have a difficult time giving an informative answer. For example, try to answer this question in 30 seconds: "What are your five major strengths?" Difficult question for you? Could you answer it in 30 seconds? Every candidate should be able to communicate their strengths. You have many more than five skills and, with appropriate preparation, you can answer a question like this easily and well.

Recruiters will want to know many things about you. Here are some categories to prepare for:

Skills and Abilities	Interests	Extracurricular Activities
Past Work Experience	GPA	Values
Personality Characteristics	Achievements	Goals

Be prepared to answer (and discuss) questions concerning these areas. Think about what questions the recruiter may ask and prepare to answer them. Practice answering the 40 frequently asked questions on the next pages until you are confident you can answer them during an interview. Based on your answers to questions like these, the recruiter will gather the information needed to make an employment decision.

40 Questions Frequently Asked During the Employment Interview

As reported by 92 companies surveyed by
Frank S. Endicott, Director of Placement, Northwestern University

1. What are your future vocational plans?
2. In what school activities have you participated? Why? Which did you most enjoy?
3. How do you spend your spare time? What are your hobbies?
4. What type of position most interests you?
5. Why do you think you might like to work for our company?
6. What jobs have you held? How were they obtained and why did you leave?
7. What courses did you like best? Least? Why?
8. What percentage of your college expenses did you earn? How?
9. How did you spend your vacations while in school?
10. What do you know about our company?
11. What qualifications do you have that make you feel you'll be successful in your field?
12. What extracurricular offices have you held?
13. If you were starting college all over again, what courses would you take?
14. Do you prefer any specific geographic location? Why?
15. Why did you decide to go to this particular school?
16. What was your high school class rank? Where will you probably rank in college?
17. Were your extracurricular activities worth the time you devoted to them? Why?
18. What personal characteristics are necessary for success in your chosen field?
19. Why do you think you would like this particular type of job?
20. Do you prefer working with others or by yourself?
21. What kind of boss do you prefer?
22. Are you primarily interested in making money or do you feel that service to people is a satisfactory accomplishment?
23. Can you take instructions without feeling upset?
24. Tell me a story.
25. How did previous employers treat you?
26. What have you learned from some of the jobs you have held?
27. What interests you about our product or service?
28. Do you feel you have done the best scholastic work of which you are capable?
29. How did you happen to go to college?
30. How did you choose your major?
31. Have you ever had any difficulty getting along with fellow students and faculty?
32. What have you done that clearly demonstrates your leadership ability?
33. Tell me about yourself.
34. What is your major weakness?
35. Are you willing to go where the company sends you?
36. What jobs have you enjoyed the most? The least? Why?
37. What are your own special abilities?
38. Would you prefer a large or a small company? Why?
39. How about overtime work?
40. What have you done which shows initiative and willingness to work?

Know about the Employer and the Job

What would you say if a recruiter asked, "What do you know about our company?" or "What about this job interests you?" Responses such as, "Well, duh, what do you do?" or "What does your company have to offer me?" would earn you a quick rejection letter. You are not prepared for an interview if you don't know about the organization and the position you are applying for.

What types of information should you know **about the employer?** The following are some of the points you may want to know prior to the interview.

EMPLOYER INFORMATION

1. What are the organization's products and/or services?
2. Where are their facilities located?
3. What is done at the facility where you will work?
4. How large is the firm or agency and how large is the facility where you will be employed?
5. What is the companies growth record (as measured by growth in sales/profits, plant expansions, increase in people employed, new markets entered, and increase in market share)?
6. What is the firm's ranking and reputation in the industry?

What types of information should you know **about the job?** At minimum, you should know what the job is and what you would do. Try to identify what you could expect to learn from working there and any special skills which you may possess that would make you more valuable to the employer.

There are many resources you can use to get organization and job information. Begin by talking with your co-op adviser, who will usually be able to tell you about the firm's position and direct you to appropriate company literature and job descriptions. If more information is needed, ask your co-op adviser where to find it. Visit the campus career library; you may find exactly what you need there. Reread the chapter in this book on Career Planning for additional resources. Finally, contact co-op students or other people who have been employed by the organization. They can tell you the "inside story."

Especially note that you will need to integrate what you know about the job and organization. You will need to combine this knowledge into answers to questions such as, "Why do you want to work for us?" You will apply knowledge about yourself and the company to form an answer that will show your interests, strong qualifications, and the match between what they have to offer and what you want to do and learn.

Mock Interview

Prior to an actual interview you should do mock interviews with a friend, your parents, or by looking in a mirror. These practice sessions should include the information and questions you have assimilated, so that you will not be caught off guard and stammer for a response in the real interview.

*Clothes don't make the man,
but clothes have got many a man a good job.*
—Herbert Harold Vreeland

Dress

Your appearance may be the first piece of information (other than your resume and portfolio) that the recruiter sees. How you look is the basis of the interviewer's first impression–and first impressions can be lasting ones.

What is proper interview attire? This question is easy to answer if you know what the recruiter is looking for in a candidate. **The recruiter wants to hire an aspiring professional.** Conservative dress is most appropriate. Suits and ties for men. Simply tailored dresses or suits for women. Make sure all clothes are clean and neatly pressed. Shoes should be shined. "Trendy" apparel is not appropriate. Keep jewelry to a minimum so it doesn't distract the interviewer. For example, women's earrings should be small and inconspicuous. (Men, don't wear the earring to an interview.) Women's makeup and perfume (and men's cologne) should be subtle, not obvious.

Plan what you wear to a job interview as carefully as you conducted the research for your resume. Design your clothing strategy to fit the company's current workforce. Gather information about the organization's history, products, and services from catalogues, promotional brochures, and annual reports. Analyze the photographs of people on-the-job to identify the company's image. (This will also enhance your ability to converse comfortably and accurately during your interview.) Quite simply, the key to dressing successfully for an interview is to present yourself in the "Image of the Company"–as if you already work there.

*Keeping your clothes well pressed will keep you
from looking hard pressed.*
—Coleman Cox

There may be some variations on the most effective way to dress for specific companies and industries. In general, there are differences in how employees dress in different fields. For example, employees in fashion-related companies, accounting firms, engineering companies, banking, and retailing adopt different clothing styles. However, there are some general guidelines you should follow in deciding what to wear for an interview, regardless of the type of company or field.

Many companies have adopted a "corporate casual" dress code for the workplace. Often they will allow for corporate casual attire in the interview. Unfortunately there is no agreement amongst employers and professionals on what dictates acceptable casual dress. Some employers allow oxford shirts and khakis for men and blouses and skirts or pants for women. While others may approve of typical college attire such as blue jeans. Since there is no regaining the "first impression" it is best to play it safe. In the interview situation, it is a good idea to follow the standard interview "uniform" and later adopt the company's accepted dress code once you have secured the position. The standard professional interview "uniform," appropriate in most business environments, is a dark suit with white shirt or blouse and sophisticated accessories. Because you are in college, financial resources may be limited. Invest in at least one excellent outfit. Choose one with clean lines and sophisticated details, and quality materials. You won't go wrong with classic tailoring reflecting current styles. Pay close attention to the all-important finishing touches: collar, cuffs, hair, jewelry, accessories and, for women, make-up.

There is new strength, repose of mind,

and inspiration in fresh apparel.
—Ella Wheeler Wilcox

Your interview outfit should be comfortable both physically and emotionally. Take the time for a trial run. Test the outfit by wearing it before the interview. Also, use this opportunity to have a "mock interview," to help you get psyched up, to build your confidence, and to solve any problems or end any anxieties about your outfit before to the interview. Don't wait until the interview to find out that you have problem fasteners, splits, and other clothing nightmares that can make you "fidgit" away a job opportunity.

The image you convey to a prospective employer is important, and part of your image is your appearance. Your appearance contributes—positively or negatively—to an interviewer's overall evaluation of you. Keep in mind that your goal is to create a positive impression of a well dressed, confident, capable soon-to-be new employee.

The following are the components of a basic wardrobe that create the right interview appearance—and prepare you for on-the-job career dressing.

Power Dressing for Men

- Tailored suit in a current style (cleaned and pressed)
- Dark (navy, gray, black)
- Excellent fit
- Wool or wool blend (lightweight or medium weight)
- Conservative blazer and pants (if no suit is available)
- White or pale blue shirt (shirts must be ironed)
- Tie should be classic, small patterned print
- Dark, polished shoes
- Jewelry (limited): tietack, traditional watch, wedding or class ring

Power Dressing for Women

- Classic, tailored suit in a current style
- Upscale blazer and skirt (skirt at or below the knee)
- Blouse or scarf that complements your outfit
- Dress:

    Classic style, quality details (no ruffles, frills, or "girlish" styles)

    Wool, silk, or linen blends

- Colors can range from blues, black, gray, tans
- Jewelry (limited): conservative earrings, watch, necklace, ring

Good clothes open all doors.
—Thomas Fuller

List of Dressing Do's and Don'ts

DO

Men	Women
Get a professional haircut	Get a professional haircut
Manicure nails	Manicure nails
Polish shoes	Polish shoes, wear low heels
Shave	Watch hemline (on knee or lower hemline)

DON'T

Men	Women
Overdress with trendy fashions	Overdress with trendy fashions
Over-accessorize	Over-accessorize
Wear earrings	Wear low-cut or revealing neckline
Wear loafers or boatshoes	Use too much make-up
Chew gum	Chew gum

THE INTERVIEWER IS EXPECTING YOUR BEST, GIVE THEM YOUR BEST.

A General Concern

By the time you actually go to the interview, you may be nervous. You have spent a lot of time perfecting your credentials. You have done some serious self-analysis, selected organizations to pursue for a co-op position, and prepared for the interview. But the opportunity to work in that special position depends on...THIS INTERVIEW! If you interview well, you may get the job. If not.... At this point, only a rock could be completely calm, cool, and collected.

Don't worry about being anxious or nervous. This is normal and even provides extra energy that will keep you alert and help you perform well during the interview. Without this energy, you might come across as "flat" or dull.

A well-trained recruiter knows you're nervous and will try to put you at ease at the start of the interview. By asking easy-to-answer questions (about campus activities or the weather, for example), the recruiter will help you relax and "warm up." As the interview proceeds, you'll forget about being nervous. As you have more interviews and learn what to expect in these situations, your anxieties will dissipate.

Interview Formats

Generally, interviews fall into four different formats:

Format 1 **Structured Interview:** organized, very formal, follows a planned script

Format 2 **Unstructured Interview:** more spontaneous, has no script, questions are generated by the candidate's responses

Format 3 **Multiple or Group:** used when the candidate is interviewed by different people at separate times or in a group; this format may be intermixed with structured or unstructured formats

Format 4 **Stress Interview:** puts the candidate on the defensive

Unfortunately, you the candidate are not able to choose the format the interviewer will use. Most often, however, as a co-op job candidate you will encounter a structured or unstructured interview.

Our greatest problems in life come not so much from the situations we confront as from our doubts about our ability to handle them.
—Susan Taylor

Interview Guidelines

There are some general guidelines to follow, things that experts say to do or not do, in order to have a successful interview and increase the probability of receiving a job offer. Following these suggestions will help you look professional, project a professional image, and communicate more effectively during the interview.

INTERVIEW DO'S AND DON'TS

DO

1. Prepare for the interview with research and mock interviews.
2. Go to bed early and get a good night's sleep.
3. Groom yourself appropriately.
4. Know the interview time, where it is, and how to get there.
5. Arrive early.
6. Use the restroom prior to the interview.
7. Know the recruiter's name.
8. Be friendly and courteous to everyone you meet.
9. Give a firm handshake.
10. Use manners.
11. Use good non-verbal skills - eye contact, posture, gestures.
12. Focus on the positive.
13. Ask questions.
14. Show enthusiasm and interest in the position.
15. Be truthful.
16. Thank the recruiter for taking the time to interview you and discuss the position.

DON'T

1. Criticize others or make negative comments about anyone or anything.
2. Smoke.
3. Chew gum, candy, or anything else.
4. Take anyone–person or animal–with you. A seeing-eye dog is the only exception to this.
5. Use profanity.
6. Wear strong perfume or cologne.
7. Mumble.
8. Apologize for low grades or other weaknesses.
9. Cry, get mad, or display strong negative emotions.
10. Ask about salary or benefits until you have a job offer.

Be especially careful to **arrive early.** Arriving 20 minutes before the interview not only gives you a cushion of time if you get delayed, but also allows you time to focus and relax. During this "extra time," use the restroom. Check the mirror to be sure you look fine–hair combed, clothes straight. This is only a quick check and clean up since you have previously taken a bath or shower, combed your hair, brushed your teeth, cleaned your nails, used deodorant, etc.

If the interview is conducted at the company or agency's facility, consider *everyone* you meet to be part of the interview process. **Be friendly and courteous.** If you are rude to the receptionist, you can kiss that job offer good-bye.

Be polite. If you interrupt during the interview, excuse yourself. Be slightly formal. Don't use the recruiter's first name unless specifically asked to do so. Don't prop your feet or elbows on the recruiter's chair or desk. "Yes, Sir" and "Yes, Ma'am" are perfectly acceptable responses. "Yeah" and "Uh huh" are not; delete these slangy terms from your vocabulary. In the rare case that the recruiter takes you to lunch, order something you know you can eat neatly and easily.

Always be truthful. The recruiter will know if you are being outright dishonest or even shading the truth. Sometimes it is obvious, sometimes it is a feeling based on experience. Whichever the case, if there is any doubt about your honesty, you will not be offered the job. Being truthful does not mean that you have to reveal all the details about a situation. You should focus on and stress positive information that presents you in the best light. Within this framework, be honest and accurate in what you do say.

Be positive in everything you do or say. Criticizing others can tag you as a "complainer," and who wants to hire a complainer? Being negative about yourself, others, experiences, or organizations conveys a negative attitude. The interviewer wants to hire a co-op with a positive attitude. Stress your strengths and emphasize the positive.

Some interviewers will discuss salary and company benefits during the interview, and others will not. If the subject is not brought up by the recruiter, do not raise it yourself. When you receive an offer of employment, it will usually include a salary offer. If not, this is the time to ask questions. If the recruiter does talk about salary and benefits during the interview and asks if you have any questions, be cautious. Asking too many–or too detailed–questions can make you sound more interested in money than in the co-op job's experience. The employer may dismiss you as a "money-grubber" who is not really enthusiastic about the learning opportunity.

Prior to an interview, review this chapter to have this information fresh in your mind. You will **feel–and be–prepared** and able to avoid many of the pitfalls that can befall you in an interview.

Interview Tips

How To Market Yourself More Effectively

So, you think your major is Accounting, Industrial Design, Mechanical Engineering...Wrong! When it comes to the interview everyone has the same major...**Marketing.** Whether your G.P.A. is 4.0 or 2.0, to get the job you must market yourself better than other candidates do. For co-op positions, you may be competing with peers from your college in your own major, students in other majors, and students from other universities and colleges across the United States and the world. The competition is tough!

During the interview, you must convince the recruiter that you have the skills, abilities, personal characteristics, values, interests, and potential that you need to perform successfully on the job. You must show that there is a good match between what the job offers and what you want to do. Finally, you must show that you are interested in the position and the organization. You indicate these attributes through your communications during and after the interview.

The following are interview tips that will help you communicate more effectively.

TIP ONE

In talking with the recruiter, use positive non-verbal behaviors. Maintain eye contact. Look at the interviewer while you are talking. Sit up. Posture is important. Smiles, head nods, body and hand gestures (yes, it is acceptable to "talk with your hands")–all can communicate positive things about you. A "lively" voice, one that changes in volume as well as pitch, communicates more effectively. By using these non-verbal behaviors, you can increase your ratings in important areas such as ability to communicate, leadership potential, enthusiasm, motivation, sociability, aggressiveness, initiative, persuasiveness, self-confidence, positive attitude, and intelligence.

TIP TWO

Expand your answers. Sometimes one- or two-word answers are appropriate. However, the recruiter rarely learns much about you from these very short answers. In addition, they make it difficult to keep the conversation going. Elaborate! Give examples of personal experiences to demonstrate a point. The interview will flow more smoothly, the recruiter will learn more, and you will increase the probability of a job offer.

TIP THREE

Ask questions. You need to learn about the organization and the job to make a good decision about the position. Questions also convey your interest in the company and the job. The rule of thumb for many interviewers is, "No questions, no job."

What kind of questions should you ask? Not ones that are clearly answered in the organization's literature that you should have read. If it looks like you did not prepare, the organization will not be not prepared to hire you. Do ask questions that will help you decide if this is the employer and the position you want. Ask questions generated by the company materials. If you tour the organization's facility, ask about what you see and what you are being told. In general, ask about things you want to know.

Prior to the interview, it may help to generate a list of questions you want to ask the recruiter. As you do, you should notice that some questions could be asked of almost any employer. You've just created a good "question base" for every interview.

- What are the most important things you would want me to learn during the first co-op work quarter?
- How might my job responsibilities change from the first to the second (or additional) co-op quarters?
- Do you sponsor any special seminars or training programs that I might attend?
- Do you hire co-op students after graduation to fill full-time positions in your organization?
- What might a typical career path be for someone with my major?

Other questions are specific to the particular position:

- Will I be using AutoCAD version 10 or 12?
- Is this position totally inside sales or will I also have the opportunity to travel and make sales trips to customers' facilities?
- Will I work in research and development during the third or fourth co-op quarter?

Use both types of questions in your interviews.

TIP FOUR

Anticipate problem areas and prepare to address those areas **if the interviewer** asks about them. **You should not** address these areas if the recruiter doesn't. Find a way to put a positive spin on them and make yourself look good.

The subject in this category most often of concern to co-op students is grade point average. Consider this situation. A student's overall G.P.A. is low but improving. In response to a question about the low G.P.A., this student could say, "When I began college, my study skills were poor, and I did not realize how much study time was required to make good grades. The last two quarters, after I began to learn what was required, I made a 2.8 and a 3.2. I anticipate at least a 3.2 this quarter."

TIP FIVE

People in sales and marketing always do three things when selling a service or product. They give a sales pitch, ask for what they want, and follow-up. This technique also works in the interview. Be prepared to **give a pitch** that will show you already have, or are developing, the skills, and other qualifications that will make you an excellent employee for the organization in the position you are seeking. Show that there is a good match between what you want to do and the potential job. **Express interest** in the position.

After the interview, usually within a day, indicate your interest and initiative by sending a "thank you" letter. (This reminds the interviewer of you.) Thank him or her for the interview, reiterate your interest in the position, give a brief review of your reaction to the information you received, and respond to or follow-up with any specific requests made during the interview. This is also the time to request any additional information you need. When an employer is unsure of which candidate to hire, the student who writes a thank you note can be the one that gets hired over those who did not bother to take the time to write and send this important piece of correspondence.

TIP SIX

As soon as possible after the interview, make notes for yourself. Write down key points about the position and the organization. Later, when you are trying to recall what you discussed during the interview, these notes will be invaluable.

TIP SEVEN

Shortly after the interview, debrief yourself. Think about what you did well in the interview and want to continue. Identify areas for improvement and devise ways to better your performance in the next interview.

Contact your co-op adviser to discuss your interviewing skills. Your adviser may be able to get feedback from the recruiter about your interview and help you better prepare yourself for the next one. To improve your skills, participate in additional mock interviews to practice and receive feedback.

IN CONCLUSION

Do not expect to receive an offer of employment from every employer that interviews you. This will not happen no matter how good you are. There are many factors that affect employment decisions. Some you can control and others you cannot. **Prepare to successfully interview every organization.** Success is measured by how well you interviewed, not by whether you got an offer from each employer. If you have enough successful interviews, you will receive job offers.

Responding to Awkward or Illegal Questions During the Interview

During the interview, the employer needs to:

1. demonstrate dignity and mutual respect for the prospective candidate,
2. ensure that questions pertain to the candidate's skills and are job related, and
3. find the best candidate for the job.

During the interviewing process, the employer is expected to be fair. Women, older individuals, the physically challenged, African Americans, Latinos, Native Americans, and other ethnic groups have faced employment discrimination in the past. Unfortunately, there is evidence that discrimination still exists in some parts of the workforce. As a prospective candidate, you should have a clear understanding of your rights and you should be knowledgeable about the current laws.

In many cases, co-op candidates will be interviewed by someone other than a human resources professional trained to be a skilled interviewer. In these cases, the interviewer (who lacks skill in this area and may be as nervous as the interviewee) may ask inappropriate questions–sometimes just to break the ice. If and when you are asked questions during an interview that seem awkward or illegal, think about your response before replying. Quickly assessing how the question makes you feel will enable you to respond appropriately. If a question feels uncomfortable, you are within your rights to refuse to answer. Examples of illegal questions include:

What is your marital status?

How old are you?

Do you have children?

What is your religious affiliation?

How much do you weigh?

It is also appropriate to advise the employer that a question is illegal. If you feel the question was asked without harmful intent or if you do not want to confront the employer, you can try a more diplomatic approach. Instead of answering an inappropriate questions, respond by directing your comments to your specific skills, interests, assets and career commitment. However you handle the situation, be sure to report such incidents to your co-op adviser.

Although it is discriminatory for an employer to request information about race, age, and other topics (or request a picture) during the interview, you may be asked (legally) to supply this kind of information after you have been hired for personnel, affirmative action, or other required reports.

OHIO CIVIL RIGHTS COMMISSION

A GUIDE FOR APPLICATION FORMS AND INTERVIEWS

PRE-EMPLOYMENT INQUIRIES: LAWFUL AND UNLAWFUL

INQUIRIES BEFORE HIRING	LAWFUL	UNLAWFUL*
1. Name	Name	Inquiry into any title which indicates race, color, religion, sex, national origin, handicap, age or ancestry.
2. Address	Inquiry into place and length at current address.	Inquiry into any foreign addresses which would indicate national origin.
3. Age	Any inquiry limited to establishing that applicant meets any minimum age requirements that may be established by law.	A. Requiring birth certificate or baptismal record before hiring. B. Any inquiry which may reveal the date of high school graduation. C. Any other inquiry which may reveal whether applicant is at least 40 years of age.
4. Birthplace, National Origin or Ancestry		A. Any inquiry into place of birth. B. Any inquiry into place of birth of parents, grandparents or spouse. C. Any other inquiry into national origin or ancestry.
5. Race or Color		Any inquiry which would indicate race or color
6. Sex		A. Any inquiry which would indicate sex. B. Any inquiry made of embers of one sex, but no the other.
7. Height and Weight	Inquires as to ability to perform actual job requirements.	Being a certain height or weight will not be considered to be a job requirement unless the employer can show that no employee with the ineligible height or weight could do the work.
8. Religion – Creed		A. Any inquiry which would indicate or identify religious denomination or custom. B. Applicant may not be told any religious identity or preference of the employer. C. Request pastor's recommendation or reference.
9. Handicap	Inquiries necessary to determine applicant's ability to substantially perform specific job without significant hazard.	A. Any inquiry into past or current medical conditions not related to positions applied for. B. Any inquiry into Workers' Compensation or similar claims.
10. Photographs	May be required after hiring for identification.	Require photograph before hiring.
11. Arrests, Convictions	Inquiries into <u>conviction</u> of specific crimes related to qualifications for the job applied for.	Any inquiry which would reveal arrests without convictions.
12. Relatives	Inquiry into name, relationship and address of person to be notified in case of emergency.	Any inquiry about a relative which would be unlawful if made about the applicant.
13. Work Schedule	Inquiry into willingness or ability to work required work schedule.	Any inquiry into willingness or ability to work any particular religious holidays.
14. Organizations	Inquiry into membership in professional organizations and office held, excluding any organization, the name or character of which indicates the race, color, religion, sex, national origin, handicap, age or ancestry of its members.	Inquiry into every club and organizations where membership is held.
15. Military Service	A. Inquiry into service in U.S. Armed Forces when such service is a qualification for the job.	A. Inquiry into military service in armed service of any country but the U.S. B. Request for military service records.

		B. Require military discharge certificate after being hired.	C.	Inquiry into type of Discharge.
16. Education		A. Inquiry into nature and extent of academic, professional or vocational training. B. Inquiry into language skills, such as reading and writing of foreign languages, if job related.	A. B.	Any inquiry which would reveal the nationality or religious affiliation of a school. Inquiry as to what mother tongue is or how foreign language ability was required.
17. Miscellaneous		Any question required to reveal qualifications for the job applied for.		Any non-job related inquiry which may elicit or attempt to elicit any information concerning race, color, religion, sex, national origin, handicap, age or ancestry of an applicant for employment or membership.
18. References		General personal and work references which do not reveal the race, color, religion, sex, national origin, handicap, age or ancestry of the applicant.		Request for references specifically from clergymen or any other persons who might reflect race, color, religion, sex, national origin, handicap, age or ancestry of applicant.
19. Citizenship		A. Whether a U.S. Citizen. B. If not, whether applicant intends to become one. C. If U.S. Residence is legal. D. If spouse is a citizen. E. Require proof of citizenship after being hired. F. Any other requirement mandated by the Immigration Reform and Control Act of 1986, as amended.	A. B. C.	If native-born or naturalized. Proof of citizenship before hiring. Whether parents or spouse are native-born or naturalized.

I. Employers acting under bona fide Affirmative Action programs or acting under orders of Equal Employment law enforcement agencies of federal, state, or local governments may make some of the prohibited inquiries listed above to the extent that these inquires are required by such programs or orders.

II. Employers having Federal defense contracts are exempt to the extent that otherwise prohibited inquiries are required by Federal law for security purposes.

III. Any inquire is prohibited although not specifically listed above, which elicits information as to, or which is not job related and may be used to discriminate on the basis of, race, color, religion, sex, national origin, handicap, age or ancestry in violation of law.

* Unless bona fide occupational qualification is certified in advance by the Ohio Civil Rights Commission.

Permission for reproduction of "Questioning Applicants for Employment and Membership in Labor Organizations - A Guide for Application Forms and Interviews," was granted by the Ohio Civil Rights Commission, Columbus, Ohio, 1994.

♦ CASESTUDY ♦
The Interview

You are the **PUBLIC RELATIONS MANAGER** for a non-profit organization. Your office is responsible for all print advertisements, posters, and brochures that promote the organization's activities as well as a monthly cable access program highlighting the programs and events your organization sponsors. It is also the responsibility of your department to work with local media to promote events and programs. Until last year, this was a one-person operation and you were definitely overloaded with work. You convinced your Director to let you hire a co-op student to assist you. You are now looking for a student to work with you next term. After carefully reviewing the resumes, you have chosen two students to interview. You are particularly interested in their responses to a few key questions. On the following pages are resumes for Jennifer Arnold and Rebecca Carter along with their answers to key questions in the interview.

Question 1: How well do you think each candidate answered the key questions? For each of the key questions, determine which candidate's answer best suits your needs as the Public Relations Manager.

Question 2: After reviewing the resumes and the candidates answers to the key questions, who do you think is best qualified for the position? Why?

Resume #1 for Public Relations Case Study

JENNIFER LEIGH ARNOLD

jarnoldl@ucmail.a&s.uc.edu

CURRENT ADDRESS
4590 Hamilton Ave. #42
Cincinnati, Ohio 45219
513-861-3376

PERMANENT ADDRESS
5398 Willow Ridge Run
Evanston, Indiana 46723
812-422-9834

EDUCATION

University of Cincinnati, Cincinnati, Ohio
College of Arts and Sciences, 1/1997 to present
G.P.A.: 3.72/4.0
Major: English Literature, Class of 2003

Evanston School for Girls, Evanston, Indiana
Valedictorian
Graduated: 6/1996

EXPERIENCE

The News Record, University of Cincinnati, Cincinnati, Ohio 9/1998 to present
Advertising Production Assistant: Responsible for design, production and layout of newspaper ads on Macintosh computers using publishing software program QuarkXPress and other design tools.

Production Assistant: Responsible for pastedown of newspaper before it is sent to the printer.

University of Cincinnati Medical Center, Cincinnati, Ohio 3/1997 to 9/1998
Video Services Co-op: Responsible for filming lectures, assisting on shoots, editing video tape, dubbing video for clients and organizing teleconferences.

Marshalls, Evanston, Indiana 9/1995 to 12/1996
Retail Merchandising Co-op: Responsible for stocking and keeping an inventory of sale and clearance items in clothing department.

SCHOLARSHIPS AND AWARDS

University Honors Scholarship; 1997-1998, 1998-1999
College of Arts and Sciences Dean's List

> **Resume #2 for Public Relations Case Study**

REBECCA M. CARTER
2445 Bethesda Lane
Cincinnati, Ohio 45243
(513) 544-2297

Education

1992-Present
University of Cincinnati, Cincinnati, Ohio
Pursuing a Bachelor of Arts in Communication and a Writing Certificate in Journalism
Current 3.0 G.P.A. Expected Graduation - June 2003

Accomplishments

* Excellent academic record in communication
* Earned 80% of college and living expenses

Work Experience

July 1998-Present
McAlpins   **Kenwood, Ohio**
Part-time sales associate for Clarins cosmetics. Sales and promotion of products. Responsible for the creation and implementation of in-store promotional events and building clientele through written and oral contact.

June 1997-Sept 1997
United Way   **Reading, Ohio**
Worked full-time on co-op assignment as Special Events Assistant. Planned and coordinated their 1st Annual Mudd Volleyball Tournament. Obtained corporate and radio sponsorship. Recruited volunteers and worked with news media in promoting the event.

Dec 1997-April 1998
Worked full-time on co-op as Teamwalk Coordinator for WalkAmerica. Responsibilities included recruitment and retention of teams from companies in the area by way of letter, telephone, and oral presentation. Created and coordinated WalkAmerica promotions. Wrote, edited, and published WalkAmerica newsletter.

Summer 1997
Party Planners   **Blue Ash, Ohio**
Began as intern and then received full-time position. Attained hands-on experience in nearly all aspects of special events production. Wrote press releases, created job proposals, assisted in artistic creations of job set-ups, and was actively involved in company promotions and advertising.

Activities

Student Government - Marketing/PR Committees
1998 & 1999 University of Cincinnati Homecoming Committee
Treasurer of Communication Association Seeking Excellence
University of Cincinnati Public Relations Officer

References

Will be forwarded upon request

Answers to Key Questions For Public Relations Case Study

Question 1

If you are hired for this position, you will be working as my assistant in the public relations department. In your mind, what does public relations mean?

Jennifer

Basically, public relations is making sure that the public likes your product or service. In a way I guess it's like customer service except you're not dealing with just one customer at a time, you're dealing with the whole world.

Rebecca

Public relations is using whatever form of non-paid advertising that you have at your disposal to get your message across to the general public. In a lot of cases, this means getting your message spread through the media. In other cases it might mean brochures, annual reports, posters, etc.

Question 2

Tell me how your past experiences have prepared you to assume a position like this.

Jennifer

Well, where I am currently working at the News Record, I have developed quite a few skills in the area of layout and design. I have done some desktop publishing as well as manual pastedown of newspaper columns. Before that I worked as a co-op for the Medical Center's video services department. We were sort of like a miniature T.V. station in that we could do everything necessary to produce a video from shooting, to editing, to dubbing. And I have developed quite a few people skills, not only with those jobs, but also as a salesperson.

Rebecca

I think that my academics have prepared me very well for a position like this. I know that a big part of public relations is writing and I have almost completed my Writing Certificate in Journalism. In my previous positions I wrote press releases and worked with the news media. I also created a newsletter to keep everyone informed about WalkAmerica. And I have prior experience in the non-profit area so I understand all the constraints and how to work within them.

Question 3

How do you work under pressure? Give me an example of a time that you had to meet a strict deadline.

Jennifer

At the News Record we are always under a strict deadline. And sometimes it's difficult because we don't get the information for the ads until the last minute. But it's never really been a problem for me. In fact I think that I might be a little more creative when I'm under the gun. I can remember one ad that I got the copy notes for just one hour before deadline. I tried not to get upset and just concentrated on getting it in on time. It turned out to be one of my best. The client even called me to thank me for doing such a good job.

Rebecca

I guess the best example that I have of that is an experience that I had with Party Planners. We were helping to promote a screening of the new Steven Speilberg film and none of the materials that we needed had arrived the day before the screening. We were all pretty upset. But I was able to get in touch with someone at the studio who overnighted us the things that we needed and everything worked out. Basically when I'm under a pressure-filled situation, I just try to make the best of things and not to get too upset.

ACTIVITY ♦ ACTIVITY ♦ ACTIVITY ♦ ACTIVITY

In-Class Interviews

This interview exercise is designed to let the class observe a job interview, give interview experience to two students, and allow the class and instructor to critique the interviews.

Central Colorado Mine Equipment, Inc.

Mid City, Colorado

Central Colorado Mine Equipment, Inc. is the manufacturer of mining safety equipment. Products include protective head gear and clothing for miners and testing equipment for mine installation. The company maintains office and manufacturing facilities in Mid City, Colorado (Pop. 200,000). Sales representatives are located in most of the mining regions in the Western United States. C.C.M.E. has been in existence for ten years and has had net profits in excess of $600,000 each of the last three years. The company is modest in size with a management/salaried staff of 20 and a labor force of 150 hourly employees.

Mid City has a diversified economy with a large white-collar workforce. In addition to C.C.M.E., several mining companies and related businesses have home offices in the city. In recent years, several high tech businesses have relocated in Mid City. There is one community college (public) and a small co-ed (private) university in the city.

You have heard informally that in recent months there has been labor unrest at C.C.M.E. and that several unions are actively recruiting the hourly employees, trying to force an election for a bargaining agent. You also know that while C.C.M.E. has shown steady growth and has been profitable the past three years, economic forecasts indicate the mining industry may be in for uncertain times. At present, however, wages paid at all levels are very good when compared to other similar corporations and industries.

You are interviewing for the newly created position of:

Assistant to the Vice President - Manufacturing

Duties include:

- Serve as chief staff assistant to the Vice President
- Prepare reports as required
- Review status and prepare monthly summary reports regarding income/expense financial data, employee productivity, and sales
- Edit monthly newsletter for employees
- Serve as the Vice President-Manufacturing representative on the Personnel Policy Committee. (Chaired by Director, Human Resources with representatives from the Vice President-Marketing, Treasurer, and Office of the President)
- Other responsibilities as assigned by Vice President-Manufacturing

Salary will be highly competitive, the benefits package is average. You are to be interviewed by the Vice President-Manufacturing. When the interview was arranged you were told you are one of three finalists being interviewed.

Tips for Conducting This In-Class Activity

Select two volunteers from the class a week in advance and get resume-type information from them. Since this is a post-graduation position, suggest that work experiences include the type of co-op experiences they hope to have by their senior year.

Select an interviewer not known by the class. A current co-op employer who knows how to interview is ideal. Give the interviewer the student information sheets in advance.

Let each student interview for 10 to 12 minutes; allow 15 to 20 minutes for discussion and critique. Be sure the critique covers the following:

- Posture and poise of student
- Eye contact and other body language
- Voice quality and articulation
- Questions answered well and not-so-well

Suggest that interviewer ask questions about:

- How applicant feels about living in Colorado (a distant state)
- Experience or education related to analyzing financial and sales data
- Human Resources experiences
- Writing skills related to company newsletter

Student may want to know more about:

- Role of Personnel Policy Committee in the corporate structure
- Kind of newsletter-people-focused (recipes, birth announcements, social happenings, theater reviews) or corporate-focused (management priorities)
- Labor unrest and role of this position, from management prospective (newsletter as a vehicle for fighting unionization, Personnel Policy Committee's role, etc.)

If these points do not arise in the interview, the instructor can point out during the critique that there are some danger signs that should be evaluated when considering this position.

Interviewing in front of a class is difficult and student interviewees should be complimented for their contribution to this activity.

CHAPTER 8

Surviving and Thriving on the Job

Successful people succeed because they learn from their failures.
—Bettina Flores

*The world is filled with willing people;
some willing to work, the rest willing to let them.*
–Robert Frost

There is a "reality shock" that hits many new employees as they enter their first permanent job. According to Hughes (1958), this shock occurs, "...because for the first time, one confronts the gap between one's expectations and dreams, on the one hand, and what it is really like to work and be in an organization, on the other hand." The co-op experience offers you a more gradual, reality-based transition from being a student to being a full-time professional in the work world. Co-op also offers you on-the-job opportunities to learn about and develop the "people skills" that are critical to success.

In most cases, the gap between expectations and workplace reality has little to do with a new employee's first attempts to apply technical learning or theory to on-the-job tasks. Instead, in most cases, "reality shock" comes from a lack of understanding of the importance of interpersonal relationships on the job. In the workplace, personal skills are often regarded as strong indicators of future success. One of your routes to success is to become aware of these interpersonal skills, to develop them, and to use them on the co-op job–and beyond–to bridge the gap between expectation and reality.

Spotlight, a publication of the College Placement Council, reported the results of a Catalyst, Inc., survey of 377 students at six U.S. colleges:

> Students have a somewhat unrealistic view of what it takes to get ahead in the world of work...they seem to perceive success and achievement at work within the context of the college experience, where superior performance on tests can be measured. Being a team player and other important workplace concepts is not part of students' reality. Getting along with the boss, having a helpful adviser, working long hours, traveling for the job, and playing office politics were rated as less important.

The National Business Employment Weekly featured similar findings from two long-term studies, one conducted by Stanford University and the other by AT&T. Both studies tracked students to identify predictors of their future business success. The key skills-for-success that emerged from both studies were interpersonal ability, communication skills, and leadership.

Research consistently finds that interpersonal skills are highly desired competencies in the workplace. In preparation for conducting a survey, *Higher Education's Effectiveness in Preparing Students for Professional Practice: Perspectives from the Aerospace and Banking Industries,* researchers reviewed a wide variety of past research on success competencies. Four categories emerged:

- knowledge of field
- job skills (leadership, adaptability, assertiveness, critical thinking)
- interpersonal skills (communicate, understand self and others, image management and ability to project a point of view)
- work attitudes (honesty, tolerance, work habits, industry knowledge, job interest)

The emphasis on success skills is not just a long-term career issue or a research topic. As a co-op student, you will quickly encounter the importance of understanding and demonstrating these skills on your co-op assignments. As part of the contribution to the learning experience, your cooperative education employer is required to evaluate your performance on the job. Many co-op employers have designed and use evaluation forms that include areas they regard as critical in the assessment of performance. Two major corporations in the Cincinnati area include the following categories on their forms:

- communication skills
- task management
- working with others
- initiative and motivation
- understanding of technical field

General Electric Aircraft Engines, a major co-op employer, includes these categories:

- team player/interaction with others
- judgment/decision-making ability
- technical/analytical ability
- attitude/application to work
- ability to learn
- quality of work

In other words, your interpersonal skills are important to your success in the workplace beginning with your first co-op experience and continuing throughout your career. Learning on the job is the basic premise of cooperative education, as important today as it was in 1906 when Herman Schneider started cooperative education. Over the nearly 90 years that cooperative education has existed, educators and employers have built on this basic premise by identifying, articulating, and teaching co-op students the skills and competencies necessary for success. Employers then and now emphasize the importance of learning these skills and competencies, applying them on the job, and continuing to develop them throughout your career. This chapter gives a brief overview of some of how these skills apply to the workplace and things you should consider for not only surviving but thriving.

The world is filled with willing people;
some willing to work, the rest willing to let them.
–Robert Frost

Basic Survival Techniques:
The Minimum Requirements to Keep a Co-op Job

There are some basic, unwritten rules that organizations expect all employees, including co-ops, to know. Even if your supervisor never discusses these rules, you **will** be expected to follow them. They include:

Be reliable

People must be able to depend on you whether it is related to finishing a job on schedule or behaving professionally. Regular attendance and being on time are mandatory on the job. An excuse that might be acceptable for being late or missing a class will not placate an angry boss who needed you when you were not there. Be at work on time, even a few minutes early, and arrive ready to work. And remember, you are expected on the job every day, whether you think "nothing much is going on" or not.

Be Willing To Work

You're expected to work to earn your salary. Willingness to work means more than just coming in when you should and doing what you are told accurately and quickly. It means taking on extra work when there is a bottleneck, working late when there is a rush, and cheerfully accepting additional responsibilities, as you grow in usefulness to the firm. You don't always get paid overtime for these "extra" assignments–but they can lead to raises and promotions. And they are expectations, not options.

If you must be late or if you are ill and must be absent, be sure to notify your supervisor in advance (if possible) or no later than the time you are expected. Give a precise and accurate explanation. No one can destroy your integrity except yourself.

Be Self-Motivating

Working at a job is not like going to school. Evaluations are generally done quarterly for co-ops, but there are no "pop quizzes" or "mid-terms" to give you feedback. A good supervisor will keep you informed, but not all supervisors are perfect. In fact, most students will not get the amount and frequency of feedback on their performance that they have come to expect from their academic experiences. You will need to seek out feedback and monitor your own performance between official evaluations.

What makes you think the world owes you something?
–Gwendolyn Brooks

Deal with yourself as an individual worthy of respect and make everyone else deal with you the same way.
—Nikki Giovanni

Be Respectful

Show respect for yourself and others. You show respect for yourself as well as your colleagues when you look and dress neatly. Recognize that office formality, routines, and cultural norms are important. As a general rule, interact with others formally unless and until you are told to do otherwise. College-style informality may be regarded as brash and immature. Address supervisors and older managers as "Mr.," " Ms.," or "Mrs." unless you are specifically asked by the individual to use his or her first name. It is also acceptable to how an individual prefers to be addressed.

Observe Office Customs

Watch other employees and take your cues for behavior from them. If nobody takes a coffee break, do not complain or talk about how coffee breaks are allowed in another company. If you are told you can take 45 minutes for lunch, do not take more. Your friends at other companies may have three breaks a day and can take two-hour lunches, but they do not work for your boss. Office customs about breaks and lunch do not always match the formal rules. Observe the customs to fit into the work environment. Flaunting office customs is a quick way to make enemies and attract negative attention.

Keep Your Job and Social Life Separate

Your job is not an extension of your social life. Don't perch on anyone's desk. Don't take up your co-workers' or the boss's time with your private problems. Keep personal phone calls to a minimum, even if they are tolerated. And don't try to make dates in the office (see Chapter 11, Sexual Harassment).

Nothing is a waste of time if you use the experience wisely.
—Rodin

All Assigned Work Is Important

Take the attitude that all assigned work is important, and never display the attitude that an assignment is a waste of time. Those who perform routine tasks well will get opportunities to do more important work. Idea people are a dime-a-dozen; "doers" are a much rarer breed. Every task will add to your total perspective. Here's how:

- Doing some routine tasks will give you empathy for others doing similar tasks. As a co-op graduate, you are likely to advance to a leadership position where it will be important to understand the functions and problems of subordinates.

- All jobs, even at the executive level, contain some routine, even undesirable tasks. Those who adjust to and fulfill all aspects of their work are given the opportunity to advance to better positions and assignments. Realize that even the boss has unpleasant tasks (firing people, for example).

Look Carefully–and Closely–Before You Criticize

A major judgment error often made by new or inexperienced employees is not looking carefully or closely before leaping into the role of critic. The new employee may encounter policies that seem foolish, systems that seem to need improvement, or procedures that seem wasteful. Although the newcomer's first impression *may* be correct, it's important to take a second and even a third look before sharing criticism. Ask if you know all the variables. Procedures or duties that seem inefficient or even unnecessary may be more complicated than they first appear. Before running to the boss to explain how you would improve things (and prove how smart you are), watch and wait. Ask questions before you offer answers. As you learn more about systems, you may discover there are good reasons for how they are designed. If you hold your tongue now, you won't feel foolish later. After you've looked closely and carefully at a situation, and collected more information, you may be able to suggest a legitimate improvement or short cut. Discuss your observations with your supervisor and offer your suggestions tactfully. Putting your ideas on paper before discussing them can help organize your thoughts.

He that is good for making excuses is seldom good for anything else.
–Benjamin Franklin

Understand and Observe the Hierarchy

Your immediate supervisor may be a small fish in a big pond, but your supervisor is still your boss-and you are an even smaller fish in the same pond. Do not go over or around your supervisor to get noticed, to get ahead, or to complain. You will gain only negative attention from your supervisor and others. Learn and follow the chain-of-command. Develop the skills to work effectively with and for your supervisor.

Following these basic rules will help you survive in most organizations. They will serve you well throughout your career. In fact, these are rules that have endured for some time, as illustrated by this quote:

In a recent analysis of over 4,000 cases, it was found that 62 percent of the employees discharged were rated unsatisfactory because of social unadaptability, only 38 percent for technical incompetence.

This quote is from *Elements of Human Engineering,* published in 1932.

Techniques for Thriving on a Job:
How to Develop a Successful Career

The preceding section gave the basic rules for survival on your co-op jobs and beyond. But most people care about thriving, not just surviving, on the job. According to Hagberg and Leider (1982), motivated people want "good work," not just a "good job." A good job is often defined as clean, high paying, secure, and prestigious. But good work is something more: "Good work is often defined as 'integrated'–something in which who you are and what you do fits together congruently."

"Good work" yields a number of rewards. It gives you a personal identity and the feeling that you matter as an individual. It makes you feel you contribute to society, that your work is valued and needed by others. Good work also provides a multitude of opportunities to develop interpersonal relationships through interaction and communication. Because of this social aspect of work, people often speak of organizations as their "families." Finally, while work has a fundamental economic meaning–it is how you earn your living; the money earned from work can also have symbolic importance. For many people, their earnings symbolize power, achievement, security, success, or recognition.

Whichever reward is important to you, having "good work" requires more than *surviving* on a job–it demands *thriving* in your career. Thriving depends on your knowing, understanding, and implementing the key success-producing perspectives, attitudes, and behaviors described in this section.

Successful People Set Goals

Why is setting goals so important? Most people want to do the best work they can and to improve their job performance. However, the pressures of everyday life often prevent us from paying enough attention to improvement. In other cases, we feel that we have little control over our work life, so we don't try to improve. And sometimes we are discouraged by our own weaknesses or human failures. It is often easier to simply drift from task to task, without trying to get any better or improve our circumstances.

Setting goals is a way to keep your attention focused on improving on-the-job. Having an objective helps you direct your energy. Consider driving a car. If you have a destination in mind, you can use the car's energy to cope with most barriers to your progress. For example, if a road is blocked, you can choose to turn off the engine and save gasoline while you wait for the road to be reopened, or you can choose to drive along an alternate route. Through these planned responses to the environment, you will eventually arrive at your destination. However, if you begin driving with no destination in mind, you are likely to change direction randomly each time you encounter a barrier. While your ear used just as much gasoline as in the previous situation, your odds of arriving at a desirable destination are small and the odds of becoming completely lost are great.

When you have a clear goal, you can direct your energy toward attaining that objective and avoid scattering your energy in other directions. You can start planning steps to take to attain your goal and avoid unplanned or unthinking steps that take you away from it. Of course, like driving a car, directing your energy toward a specific objective doesn't mean you'll never have to make a detour or never encounter delays. However, if you know your destination, you can proceed on course as soon as possible.

Moreover, if you set goals and direct your activities accordingly, you know you charted the course you are on yourself. You will have a sense of being in control. In addition, having an objective clearly in mind enables you to know when you have succeeded. This seems obvious, but it is an important benefit of setting goals. "Success" is a term that most people use but never really define in their own minds. As a result, you can accomplish many tasks, receive many promotions, earn lots of money, and be recognized with awards–and still not feel "successful." This can occur if you don't know what "success" means to you.

Setting goals is a way to define "success" for yourself in a way that allows you to recognize your own successes, to be proud of them, and to be motivated to set new objectives and strive for new successes. In other words, you not only are successful, but you realize and experience the pleasures of your success.

The advisers guiding you through your co-op work and learning experiences recognize the value of setting goals. Some of you will be required to set goals as part of your guided work-based learning. Whether required or not, setting career goals is a way to direct your life toward your definition of success.

There is only one success–to spend your life in your own way.

–Christopher Morley

Develop the Success Skills

Your understanding of the nuances of organizational relationships can determine the course of your career. Here are some tips about these career-determinants:

Understand the Dynamics of Organizations

First, understand the system you're joining–the organization. According to Tortoriello, Blatt, and Dewing, "An organization is a social grouping that establishes task and/or interpersonal patterns of relationships for the attainment of specific objectives." "Social grouping," "interpersonal patterns," and "relationships for the attainment of specific objectives" are key elements that students often overlook as they focus on a specific task. The elements highlight the importance of interpersonal interactions and understanding their dynamics.

Power is a central element in interpersonal dynamics. Power is not a dirty word; it is in fact a close synonym for "influence." According to Blatt (1985), a definition of power is: "The ability to influence the other person(s) in achieving one's goal." Blatt emphasizes that, "Power is something that is given to one person by another. It is a person giving influence over them…It is relational, i.e., it stems out of relationships; it is not a *thing.*"

Since achieving goals with the help of others is integral to the definition of both power and an organization, knowing who is likely to have, power and why, is vital to getting tasks accomplished and to avoiding problems. Think of power as a form of currency. For example: Person A has a resource Person B wants. But whether and at what cost Person A gives that resource depends on the balance of power between A and B. According to Blatt, power springs from four sources:

Resource Control

Control of economic resources such as a salary, a travel budget, or funds to purchase a new computer; also, economic power that is part of a formal position or role such as supervisor, president, or comptroller.

Intimacy

Human beings need nurturing, caring, and love. Those who provide the intimacy that other individuals need or desire have influence over the recipients.

Expertness

Having knowledge, skill, talent, or expertise that others need produces power.

Interpersonal Linkage

Association with others who, whatever the reason, have power confers a certain degree of power. For example, relatives of the President of the United States or those who lunch with the supervisor derive power from their linkage with those who have power.

Build a Network

Building a network is a crucial component of developing success skills, discussed in Chapter 9.

There is no knowledge that is not power.

–Ralph Waldo Emerson

Learn Appropriate Interpersonal Skills

The importance of interpersonal relationships is addressed earlier, but here are some especially relevant guidelines for behavior that will help you thrive, not just survive:

- Be thoughtful of others. Be courteous, considerate, and tactful in your interactions with other employees. Be aware of cultural differences (see pages).

- Show respect for older people. Don't stereotype people as conservative and traditional just because they are older. Young people do not have a monopoly on good values or brains. In fact, new college graduates are sometimes as stubborn in their beliefs and values as they accuse others of being.

- Be modest. The quickest way to lose respect is to sound or act like a know-it-all. People will be more receptive to your ideas when you prove that you are open-minded and are conscientiously searching for the best way or the right answer.

- Know when to question the work of others or to make suggestions of a critical nature. Before speaking, make sure you understand the whole problem, and equally important, make sure the timing is right.

- Be receptive to constructive criticism. No one is perfect and you have faults equally as bad as the ones you see in others. If you cannot accept constructive criticism, why should anyone listen to your opinions? Work hard at learning to accept criticism; everyone receives it. Learn to distinguish between criticism of your performance on a task and criticism of you as a person. Constructive criticism is helpful to learning, even if a supervisor gives criticism a little too bluntly or forcefully for your taste.

- Learn to tolerate frustration. Solving problems, working with complex situations, and interacting with fellow employees, subordinates, and bosses can be frustrating. Things don't always go as smoothly as those case studies you've had in courses. Don't vent your frustrations through emotional outbursts or shows of temper. Employees are evaluated on how well they can control frustrations and whether they confront problems maturely and directly.

- Be cooperative in your relationships with your supervisor and other employees. Practice good human relations. Co-workers will cover one error in judgment, but if you are continually critical of them, they will be waiting for your mistakes.

- Be willing to accept the negative aspects as well as the opportunities of responsibilities. Don't blame "them" when something is not done correctly (incompetent subordinates or management or the system). Blaming "them" is a crutch, an alibi for your own shortcomings. Instead, take action to correct problems that are within your responsibilities. And word soon gets around on this type of unethical practice. Besides, "they" can't always be to blame.

- Recognize that you are an "outsider" coming into the organization. You may represent a threat to some of the people, particularly those with whom you will be competing for higher positions in the organization. Don't try to change things right away. "Come on slow" with other people and try to earn their trust, confidence, and respect. Most people in an organization will accept you if you modestly demonstrate that you have something to offer. Avoid the extremes of either trying to force yourself on people or being a loner. Act normally and do what you can to win friends among the majority of people.

An error doesn't become a mistake until you refuse to correct it.

–Orlando A. Battista

Develop a Positive Attitude Toward Your Work

Psychologist John Brantner recommends the following attitude:

When we are depressed or discouraged or anxious,
When we are embarrassed or ashamed,
When we are taken by surprise
These are the three surest signs
That we are in a situation
That offers the opportunity for growth.

Successful people see events at work as both challenges and opportunities while their less successful colleagues regard the same events as only problems. Your attitude determines how you approach tasks and influences your superiors' perception of you. To show your positive side, remember:

- Your attitude when an unusual demand is made on you is important. All jobs have their undesirable aspects–and every employee receives assignments that are boring or difficult. If you show resentment toward a required task, you might as well refuse the task from your supervisor's point of view. In other words, you have to do the job anyway, but lose credit because of your attitude. On the other hand, if you graciously accept an undesirable but necessary task, you turn the situation into an opportunity to advance your standing. Your supervisor, who knows when a task is not particularly desirable, will appreciate and value your positive attitude, which makes the situation easier for everyone.

- Learn all you can about the organization–customers, products and services, office operations, policies, market strategies, organizational structure, and recent history.

- Take the initiative–act on your own sense of responsibility without being prompted, urged, or directed. In other words, do more than you are asked. Volunteering for an unpopular task is an excellent way to show initiative. Practically every job offers the opportunity to show initiative, but many never see this possibility. Recognizing and acting on these opportunities is one way to show that you have the essential qualities for advanced responsibilities.

- Evaluate your progress at the end of an experience. Then, being the process of learning and evaluating all over again. All development, but especially work-related growth and learning, is a continuous cycle of learning activities. The completion of one learning experience should naturally lead to the beginning of another that builds on the results of the previous learnings. Evaluation of what you know and what you still need and want to learn is an ongoing process.

Experience is a hard teacher because she gives the test first, the lesson afterwards.
–Vernon Sanders Law

Summary

An experienced corporate human resources director, Patrick Mastery, has decades of experience watching people succeed and fail. His advice to co-op students, based on his observations, concisely summarizes this chapter:

- Make certain you understand the expectations your boss and your organization have of you...then try to exceed them.

- Be enthusiastic.

- Develop communication skills up and down the organization, but especially sideways.

- Know the business, as much of it as you can, apart from your own job.

- Learn the organization "culture" –what is acceptable, what isn't.

- Responsibility–take it on, follow through. Do what you say you are going to do.

- Politics–they may not be natural to you, but learn to live in a political arena.

- Honor the chain-of-command, communicate clearly with others, be aware of your behavior and its possible effect on others.
- Team abilities are becoming more important than individual decision-making.
- See challenging issues as opportunities, not problems.
- Start networking–maintaining and nurturing relationships. This should be an ongoing process and career skill, not a "use people when I need them" activity. Continually widen your circle.
- Be aware of self-imposed boundaries that stifle creativeness.
- Control your attitude–don't let someone else do it. Attitude = a voluntary mental condition with regard to a fact.
- You are responsible for yourself and your own career development. Don't expect others to take responsibility for your future. Spend time with your boss, career development, and human resource people for help on how to advance.
- Don't just rely on your boss or the organization to provide motivational systems; provide them to yourself.
- Understand that in any encounter you are being judged and evaluated by others.
- Don't try to change the world all at once. Go for singles, not always home runs.
- Maintain ethical conduct. In vast majority of organizations, unethical conduct will not be tolerated. It may cost you a career.
- Accomplishments count for more than the hours you put in.
- Have fun, make your own fun. If you're not having fun, you're in the wrong job.

♦ CASE STUDY ONE ♦

Job Success or Failure

Betty and the ABF Company

Betty, a co-op, has been working for ABF Company for three quarters. This work quarter has been very slow in her department, and she has really tried hard to keep busy. Today, she went to her boss to ask for more work and was told there would be no new assignments for two days. Upon asking her boss what she should do until more work was assigned, Betty was told, "Read the company's literature and review the Johnston account in order to better acquaint yourself with some of the more recent developments." Betty read the literature, reviewed the account, and found herself stuck with rest of the afternoon free...nothing left to do. The next day looked just as boring...nothing to do then either. She picked up the newspaper and began reading...There was nothing else to do.

Was Betty's response to the situation appropriate?

Why?

What are the issues involved?

What are the alternatives?

♦ CASE STUDY TWO ♦

Job Success or Failure
Bruce and Mr. Jones

Bruce has been co-oping with ABF, Inc. for two quarters. He shares an office with Mr. Jones and a number of other employees. Ms. Smith, Bruce's supervisor, has her own office and rarely comes into "The Pit," as Bruce's office is affectionately called.

Mr. Jones has "the gift of gab" and spends most of his time talking to other employees. Mr. Jones gets little work done and has the reputation of being a royal pain in the rump. Today, Bruce has the dubious honor of having Mr. Jones' attention. Mr. Jones has been talking to Bruce for 20 minutes and appears to be ready to continue for a least an hour. Bruce has been trying to work while Mr. Jones is talking but finds the talking unbearable. Bruce has never been able to concentrate when there was a lot of noise.

What might Bruce do to terminate this unbearable situation?

What issues are involved?

♦ CASE STUDY THREE ♦

Job Success or Failure

Bruce's Evaluation

Bruce is working for ABF, Inc. It is his first work quarter and he is having his 1 1/2 month work evaluation which will be followed in 1 1/2 months by his final evaluation for the co-op quarter. Bruce has been working hard, striving to do all that is required of him. Mr. Smith, Bruce's supervisor, sits down and tells Bruce, "Bruce, we have a problem here. You don't seem to be doing what is expected of you. Not only that, but you rarely take the initiative to do more than just what is expected of you."

What issues are involved here?

What does Bruce say?

What can Bruce do to avoid this type of evaluation in the future?

How might this situation have been avoided?

♦ CASE STUDY FOUR ♦

Job Success or Failure

Case Four: Bruce and the Project Deadline

Bruce, a co-op student, and two full-time employees, John and Jeff, are working on a project for their supervisor, Mr. Smith. The project was divided into three areas and each employee was assigned a specific part of the project to complete.

The deadline for completion of the project is approaching. Bruce and John have been working very hard on their parts of the project and will have them completed before the deadline. Jeff, however, has been loafing on the job and has not made much effort to complete his part of the project. It is obvious that Jeff's part will not be completed on time. Bruce and John fear that if the project is not completed on time, it may reflect negatively upon them.

What are the issues involved?

What options might Bruce and John have in dealing with this situation?

♦ CASE STUDY FIVE ♦
Job Success or Failure
Case Five: The Co-op Calendar

Bob was hired to a co-op work assignment for the Winter Quarter, which begins December 29 (according the official co-op calendar). However since his exams ended December 12, Bob and his co-op employer arranged for him to begin work on the following Monday on December 15. This worked out great for Bob's employer because the office was very busy. It would also give the present co-op an opportunity to train Bob a couple of weeks and transfer co-op duties. At the same time, Bob looked forward to earning some additional holiday money. Bob worked hard, learned a lot, and won the respect of his employer.

Bob has been invited to go to Florida for Spring Break, which begins on March 23 and ends March 27. The official practice quarter also ends on March 27. Bob's employer has indicated that Bob is needed at the office until March 27. Bob contends that since he started working two weeks early, he should be allowed to have Spring Break off. Bob's alternate co-op is not scheduled to begin work until March 29, the official first day of the Spring Practice Quarter.

What are the issues here?

What should Bob's employer do?

What should Bob do?

How should the co-op adviser handle this conflict?

♦ CASE STUDY SIX ♦

Job Success or Failure

Case Six: Computer Usage

Betty's co-op position requires use of her computer most of the day. She often receives memos and other instructions from her co-workers and supervisor through the company's email system. While Betty was working she received an email from a friend. Opening it caused her computer to become infected with a computer virus. Many important files were deleted from her computer as well as others on the network. Further inspection of Betty's computer files detected several email documents and downloads that were not work-related.

Was Betty's behavior appropriate?

How should Betty's supervisor handle this situation?

Should this situation be brought to the co-op adviser's attention?

Discuss some to the ramifications to using company equipment for personal use.

SECTION THREE

Routes to Success on the Co-op Job and Beyond

*My darkness has been filled with the light of intelligence,
and behold, the outer day-lit world
was stumbling and groping in social blindness.*
-Helen Keller

CHAPTER 9

Networking:

Using People

in the Best Sense

I am not a special person. I am a regular person who does special things.

—Sarah Vaughn

The Concept of Networking

Networking is an age-old skill that has recently been attracting more interest. It is the practiced habit of linking yourself with other people for the purposes of exchanging and evaluating information, obtaining advice, and learning and possibly growing together. Networking is a shared activity. Contrary to what many people want to believe, who you know counts as much as *what* you know in the business world. The benefits of connecting with people inside and outside your work organization can apply to seeking a job, accomplishing a task, progressing in your career, or establishing future resources for projects or problem solving.

Because networking is a *skill* that can be learned through training and/or practice, it is available to all who are willing to put forth the effort. Dr. Adele Scheele, author of *Skills for Success,* describes networking with words such as positioning, risk linking, connecting, and catapulting (using people in the *best* sense). She states, "...[networking] is a way to promote ourselves through contact with others, thereby increasing our capacity to grow into a new position."

According to Scheele, networking is an ongoing process through which social contacts, business associates, friends, and family members can connect you to others who can be of help in your career development. Networking is a *verb*. It involves time and effort, but it also involves interesting people, expanding horizons, and beneficial results. It is a skill that includes and requires not only preparation, building, monitoring, modifying, maintaining...but above all...an appreciation for the interdependence of persons. Networking is to career discovery as listening is to communication...each is the most important skill in its respective area, but at the same time the most neglected one.

The Process of Networking

When Do You Network?

Most people think of networking in relation to job hunting, but that is only one of many times when this skill comes into play, At any phase of your career development, you can make effective use of networking. While you are in college, you can begin building a network for your search for a permanent job upon graduation. During the actual job search, you can expand your network with the various contacts and interactions with different companies. Once you have a permanent job, maintaining your expanded network will help you keep current with your career field. Your network becomes an important resource of information and people, whether you are working on specific projects, exploring next steps in your career, or building bridges to future positions. Your network can be a critical source of support and information when you are exploring a possible career change. Networking is also useful in mentoring or teaching situations.

In its most effective and best sense, networking becomes a life-long building process, not just a sporadically used career tool.

Where Do You Network?

The answer to this question is simple: anywhere. At work, in social situations, within your extended family, during school or continuing education classes and seminars, at sporting events–the list can go on and on. Your network can include mentors, alumni, teachers, coaches, sponsors, experts in your field, and just plain friends who support and encourage you if the going gets rough. The only boundaries are your own creative thinking, your efforts, and your willingness to initiate conversations and pursue topics and future contacts.

How Do You Network?

Since the opportunities for networking are all around you, you need to be prepared to recognize and to respond to them. Building a network requires feeling comfortable contacting strangers, initiating conversations, looking for common ground, and asking questions. This is easier to do when you recognize that most people enjoy being questioned or interviewed to become part of a network. As A. J. Liebling said, "...there is almost no circumstance under which an American doesn't like to be interviewed...We are an articulate people, pleased by attention, covetous of being singled out."

This "singling out" can occur in informal settings (parties, conferences, meetings) or formal ones (pre-arranged informational interviews). Whatever the setting, you need to know what the rules are, how to get the information you need, *and* how to leave the impression you want. As Susan RoAne, author of a book on networking, explains, this means knowing "how to work a room" and how to "successfully manage the mingling" in informal settings. In formal settings, it means knowing how to arrange and conduct interviews with the right people. And, in all settings, you need to know when and how to probe for more information, when and how to offer information about yourself, and how to follow-up.

Networking can enrich your life and career through enlarging your circle of meaningful human connections, which can broaden your entire perspective and repertoire regarding how to meet the challenges of developing your life and career.

Acting on a good idea is better than just having a good idea.

–Robert Half

The Ingredients of Networking

Networking can be done in all the domains of your life:

Family	Spiritual
Community	Health
Work	Self-Development
Recreation	Relationships

Networking should incorporate:

- Becoming comfortable letting others know how competent you are
- Putting your best foot forward
- Frankly acknowledging your abilities
- Showing others you are a good resource for their network
- Building bridges to the future

Examples of Networking Actions

initiating	cultivating
encouraging	maintaining
developing	evaluating
promoting	pruning

Examples of Possible Results

inside information	confidential sharing
advice and ideas	a sounding board
leads and referrals	feedback
moral support	evaluating

Ability is of little account without opportunity.
—Napoleon Bonaparte

CHAPTER 10

Responding to the Reality of a Transcultural World

Being able to conduct business across geographical borders and cultural boundaries is becoming a required job skill for many employees...not just those who plan to work in a corporation's overseas office. As American corporations move into the "global" economy, employers are demanding internationally savvy employees...people with cross-cultural skills and adaptability who can communicate and work with people in other countries.

–*Spotlight,* College Placement Council, Inc., Newsletter

It takes two men to make one brother.

–Israel Zangwill

The global economy is no longer a futuristic concept, it is the reality of the present. You need to prepare yourself for this reality as you get ready to enter the professional work world, particularly if you want to enhance your opportunities to move ahead on the job. The workplace, including the co-op workplace, is culturally diverse in the United States as well as in the international arena. One function of the business world must be to provide "corrective lenses." That is, increasing cultural awareness, providing information, and teaching skills that build bridges between people. Responding to the reality of a transcultural world does not mean eliminating cultural styles and differences. It does mean learning to manage and celebrate differences in order to tap into the strengths of diversity.

Definitions

Culture is a point of view, a frame of reference, a collection of all that we are, the "lens" through which we see the world. The study and understanding of culture involves anthropology, communication, psychology, and sociology. Following are some definitions from *Webster's Dictionary* that are relative to the discussion of culture:

Acculturation	Modification of one culture as a result of contact with a different, especially more advanced culture.
Bicultural	Of or pertaining to two distinct cultures in one nation or geographic region (or person).
Culture	Sum total of ways of living built up by a group of human beings and transmitted from one generation to another; the behaviors and beliefs characteristic of a particular social, ethnic or age group.
Enculturation	Process by which the culture of a particular society is instilled in a human being from infancy onward.
Generalization	Inference of a general principle from a few facts or cases; proposition asserting something to be true of all members, or indefinite part of the members of a group, or organization, or a culture.
Intercultural	Between, among; in the midst of, mutual; reciprocal.
Multicultural	Pertaining to, of, or designed for several cultures.
Sojourner	Temporary resident alien.
Stereotype	Oversimplified, standardized conception or image of a person or class thought to typify or conform to a fixed, settled, or unvarying pattern; lacking individuality.
Transculturation	Cultural change induced by the introduction of elements of a foreign culture.

*The greatest and noblest pleasure which men
can have in this world is to discover new truths, and the
next is to shake off old prejudices.*
—Frederick the Great

A Kaleidoscope of Perspectives

Because of the rapidly developing demand for increased cultural awareness and communication skills, many resources focusing on these areas have become available. The basic essence of eight creative approaches to addressing the concept of effective cultural communication is offered here as food for thought. Just as turning the kaleidoscope presents different views of a multi-colored pattern, these authors offer different views of the multi-patterned living of a transcultural world.

Bridging Differences: Effective Intergroup Communication

W. Gudykunst (1991)

People in any culture generally behave in a regular way because of the norms, rules and values of their culture. This regularity allows cultural information to be used in making predictions.

Working Together: How to Become More Effective In A Multicultural Organization

Dr. George Simons (1989)

Culture is how we are raised to view and practice life. It is the inevitable result of rubbing elbows with one segment of the human race. It shows up in how we make, do and celebrate things. You can see it in how we talk to ourselves about "us" and "them." It tells us who "we" are and gives us attitudes about "them," and people who are different from us. It tells us what should be important as well as how to act in various situations.

Communication Between Cultures

Samovar and Porter (1991)

Culture...a concept that is not only complex but...has the potential to include nearly everything...culture provides structure that:

- ♦ enables us to make sense of our surroundings
- ♦ gives meaning to events, objects, and people in the environment
- ♦ makes the world a less mysterious place
- ♦ provides a predictable world for an individual
- ♦ provides common behaviors and definable settings
- ♦ offers a common blueprint for all of life's activities

Make Haste Slowly: Developing Effective Cross-Cultural Communications

Donald K. Smith (1984)

Culture is a pattern:

- for survival
- to improve one's life
- for relationships with other people
- for relationships to our total environment

Culture is a learned behavior, to meet challenges and needs. It is an ability to use the world surrounding us. There are four levels of culture:

Behavioral level: visible, observable actions and artifacts at the surface–personal and group actions, objects made and used, language spoken (elements we can observe that do not necessarily explain behavior).

Authority level: observable in its effects, but part of invisible culture. Most actions rest on standards maintained by the authorities accepted by a person most individual behavior rests on group authority. Most changes must come through the group, not individual.

Personal experience: invisible culture, how individual feels and interprets stronger than group authority. What is found to be satisfying, rewarding, or works well.

Core (basic assumptions): invisible not only to outsiders but also to social group and individual members. Unconscious belief system, not consciously learned. Core development comes through enculturation, or a process of growth, from baby to adult. Challenges to core beliefs can be met with disregard, laughter, anger (if position is insisted upon), mockery and scorn, or that the idea and the messenger must be destroyed. Often, the stronger the insistence (or, challenge to the core belief), the stronger the resistance.

Our Voices: Essays in Culture, Ethnicity, and Communication

Gonzalez, Houston & Chen (1994)

Humans are organizing beings and culture is an organizing term. They refer to:

- how we create communities
- how we participate in social activities
- what values are held

Communication constantly defines and redefines the community. Culture refers to a community of meaning and a shared body of local knowledge (not region or nation).

Mindsets

Glen Fisher (1989)

Mindsets: How we perceive, reason, and view the world. They govern how:
- events are evaluated
- decisions are made
- priorities for action are established

They also influence:
- international political relations
- implementation of development assistance policies
- conduct of international business and economic affairs

Donald N. Larson, anthropologist/writer on cultural learning

To move from being an outsider to the center (or an insider) in a new culture, one must develop three roles, step-by-step, yet inclusive.

Learner	child role–vulnerable/open; listen to establish one's self
Trader	of knowledge and insight, finding commonalities, bridging
Storyteller	share one's own way of life

*Be nice to people on your way up because you'll
meet them on your way down.*
–Wilson Mizner

Dispelling Stereotypes as a Means to Working in a Diverse Culture

Success on your co-op assignment will depend on your ability to work with a diverse group of individuals. You will come in contact with customers, clients, supervisors and co-workers that represent different ethnic, racial, religious, age and other cultural groups. You will interact with both men and women. You will interact with people who differ from you in their philosophies about life, work, politics, etc. Each person is an individual and is different from any other one–even within specific cultural groups; there are wide variations among individuals.

As stated above, culture is the sum total of a group's experiences, which constitutes the accepted way of life for the group. That means that any type of group can have a culture. For example, as a student you are part of a culture–the student culture–within which there may be a variety of subcultures. You enter another cultural when you begin working at a corporation–that organization's particular "corporate culture." Within the general corporate culture, your co-op employer will have its own cultural norms. To work effectively within your company's specific culture, you should learn as much as you can about it. This is analogous to what you should do when you meet someone from a different ethnic, racial, or geographic culture. You first must recognize that someone is from a different culture, and learn enough about that culture to interact effectively.

Once you begin interacting with members of other cultural groups, you may discover a variety of new and interesting cultural traits, however different they are from your own. These can include differences in personal interactions, language, food, methods of worship, value systems, family life, and myriad other factors. You may notice that members of other cultural groups approach work tasks from a different perspective than you. All cultural groups differ in some way from each another. Being culturally aware means not allowing your lack of knowledge or understanding of another culture to stereotype people. Remember, your culture is as different to them as theirs is to you.

Acknowledging cultural differences–and learning to appreciate them–will help you avoid the trap (and misinformation) of stereotyping. Stereotyping reduces your ability to work in teams and become a productive employee. It may also hamper your ability to accept authority from supervisors and other managers. Stereotyping costs an employer money in lost production and profits.

There are two ways of meeting difficulties; you alter the difficulties or you alter yourself meeting them.
    –Phyllis Bottome

Many companies have developed some form of training or handbook on working in a diverse environment. These companies recognize, clearly and simply, that it takes an entire company of employees working together to effectively meet its objectives. Become familiar with your company's policies and training opportunities in diversity management. If there is no formalized training program or materials, practice simple *professional courtesy* in your interactions with all individuals.

Some things that you can do to break down barriers and dispel stereotypes include:

- Be courteous. People respond to courteous people.

- Practice being sensitive. People are grateful when others try to understand them.

- Keep communication channels open. Listen to the needs of others. If you do not understand something, ask.

- Ask others if they will share information about their culture. You should be willing to share also.

- Disregard misinformation that you may have learned from television shows and other media. Learn through your own personal experiences.

- Remember that being different from anybody else gives you something different to offer. No other individual can make the exact contribution that you can. That works out great for you because no company would want all of its employees to be exactly alike.

> *We must learn to live together as brothers or*
> *perish together as fools.*
> –Martin Luther King

The following chart lists common but outdated labels that we tend to attach to people. Many of these outdated terms subconsciously foster stereotyping. Your co-op company may be one that is changing from these terms to some of the more appropriate ones provided.

Appropriate and Inappropriate Terminology That Stereotypes

INAPPROPRIATE TERM OUTDATED (OUT) OR OFFENSIVE (OFF)	PRESUMED NEGATIVE STEROTYPICAL BEHAVIOR	MORE APPROPRIATE DESCRIPTIVE TERM	PRESUMED POSTITIVE STEREOTYPICAL BEHAVIOR
Alien, Foreign, Foreigners. (Out/Off)	Subconscious Image of something or someone abnormal or unusual. Situated outside a country or place.	International people. Give nationality (e.g. French, Chinese).	Acknowledges cosmopolitan and international diversity.
Colored/Negro. (Out/Off)	Names given to people of African ancestry by Europeans. Outdated labels with negative images of the past.	African American, Black, Black American, African. Give nationality if not from U.S.A. (e.g. Haitian, Nigerian).	Acknowledges African and/or American Heritage. More descriptive.
Disabled/ Handicapped. (Out/Off)	Gives subconscious image of complete incapacitation.	Physically challenged. People with disabilities. Differently-able.	Acknowledges the capabilities of individuals.
First World, Second World, Third World. (Out/Off)	Gives subconscious connotation of inferiority of the people and their associated countries.	"The West", Western Countries, "The East', Eastern Bloc, Developing Countries/Nations	Gives more attention to countries location and to the political and economic situation.
Girls/Boys (Out/Off)	Gives connotation of young, immature individual incapable of making a contribution and professional decisions.	Females, Ladies, Women/Males, Gentlemen, Men.	Acknowledges maturity through years and personal and professional growth. Capableness.
Indian (Out/Off).	Name given by Europeans. Conjures a negative mental picture of savagery.	Native American.	Acknowledges the fact that group with a legitimate culture was the first to inhabit America.
Jew (Out/Off)	As adjective, disparaging.	Jewish.	Gives deference to the religion and to the cultural heritage.
Lower Class, Middle Class, Upper Class. (Out/Off)	Gives subconscious image of inferiority or superiority in behavior patterns, abilities, and human worth.	Lower Income, Middle Income, Upper Income.	Indicates income level at a certain range.
Minorities. (Out/Off)	Outdated label which gives connotation of inferiority and subordinate status.	Diverse groups, diverse populations, multicultural groups, ethnic groups.	Acknowledges the diversity and differences of groups.
Old/Aged. (Out/Off)	Gives subconscious connotation of uselessness.	Elderly, Senior Citizen.	Acknowledges years acquired and respect due. Subconsciously indicates wisdom.
Underclass. (Out/Off)	Gives subconscious connotation of inferiority in behavior and human worth.	Financially disadvantaged. Economically disadvantaged.	Indicates financial or economic picture of individual without conferring lack of social or human worth.
Whites. (Out/Off)	Often construed negatively or given with a negative undertone. Nondescript.	European American, Euro-American, White American, American Caucasian.	Acknowledges European ancestry while recognizing American heritage.

CHAPTER 11

Sexual Harassment

There is nothing more frightful than ignorance in action.
—Johann Wolfgang Von Goethe

Sexual harassment–even the term makes people uncomfortable. Perhaps it sounds too legalistic or too remote to be a real factor in a student's life. Sexual harassment is an issue that will not go away by being ignored. 20-30% of all female college students experience some form of sexual harassment (ranging from sexist comments to direct solicitation for sexual favors to assault); men can also be sexually harassed. About 5% of sexual harassment cases involve men as the victims.

Myths

Here are some myths and facts about sexual harassment.

MYTH   Sexual harassment only happens to women who are provocatively dressed.

FACT   Sexual harassment can happen to anyone, no matter how they are dressed.

MYTH   If the victim had only said "no" to the harasser, the harassment would have stopped immediately.

FACT   Many harassers are told "no" repeatedly and it does no good. "No" is too often heard as "yes."

MYTH   If you ignore sexual harassment, it will go away.

FACT   No, it won't. Generally, harassers are repeat offenders who will not stop on their own. Ignoring it may be seen as assent or encouragement.

MYTH   All men are harassers.

FACT   No, only a few men harass. Usually there is a pattern of harassment; one man harasses a number of women, sequentially, simultaneously, or both.

MYTH   Sexual harassment is harmless. People who object have no sense of humor.

FACT   Harassment is humiliating and degrading. It undermines school careers and often threatens economic livelihood. No one should have to endure humiliation with a smile.

MYTH   Sexual harassment affects only a few people.

FACT   Surveys on campus show that up to 30% of all female college students experience some form of sexual harassment. Some surveys of women in the working world have shown that as many as 70% have been sexually harassed in some way.

What Is Sexual Harassment?

Sexual harassment is primarily an issue of power, not sex. It occurs when a person with power abuses it. It is a breach of the trusting relationship that normally exists in the academic and/or work environment. Sexual harassment creates confusion because the boundary between the professional role and personal relationship blurs. The harasser introduces the personal element into what should be a sex-neutral situation.

The difference between voluntary sexual relationships and sexual harassment is that harassment contains elements of coercion, threat and/or unwanted attention in a nonreciprocal relationship. Sexual harassment usually is unwelcome and repeated behavior, but it can also be an action that only occurs once. In most normal interpersonal relationships, an individual can exercise freedom of choice in deciding with whom they wish to establish a close, intimate relationship. These choices are based on mutual attraction, caring, and reciprocal interest in pursuing the relationship. These elements are absent in sexual harassment.

Types of Sexual Harassment

Sexual harassment can involve persons in authority, co-workers, and others who make you uncomfortable because they:

- Subject you to unwanted sexual attention, such as making sexual or suggestive comments.

- Attempt to coerce you into a sexual relationship. Punish or threaten to punish you for refusal to comply.

- Imply that sexual favors may be the basis for getting a good assignment, evaluation, or promotion.

- Engage in conduct which has the purpose or effect of interfering with your performance or creating an intimidating, hostile, or offensive work or learning environment.

Simply put, sexual harassment is coerced, unethical, and unwanted intimacy.

Verbal and Physical Harassment

Most sexual harassment falls into two categories: verbal and physical.

Verbal harassment may include:

- Sexual innuendo's and comments and sexual remarks about your clothing, body, or sexual activities
- Suggestive or insulting sounds
- Humor and jokes about sex or women in general
- Sexual propositions, invitations or other pressure for sex
- Implied or overt threats

Physical harassment may include:

- Patting, pinching or any other inappropriate touching or feeling
- Brushing against the body
- Attempted or actual kissing or fondling
- Coerced sexual intercourse
- Assault

Other types of sexual harassment may include:

- Leering or ogling
- Making obscene gestures

The courts have also found that the display of sexually offensive or suggestive materials (photographs, signs, and graffiti) is a form or sexual harassment if it creates a hostile work environment.

The Effects of Sexual Harassment

Sexual harassment affects people in many harmful ways. Too often victims blame themselves. Others may also blame the victim, holding the victim responsible for what happened, rather than blaming the person who did the harassing. The victim's self-confidence and self-esteem may be diminished. Often a victim feels anger that cannot be expressed and which may lead to feelings of helplessness, powerlessness and isolation.

If You Are Sexually Harassed...

Don't Blame Yourself

Sexual harassment is not something people bring on themselves. Harassment is an action that the harasser does to someone and the victim of the behavior is not at fault. Blaming yourself only turns your anger inward and can lead to further stress and even physical and mental illnesses. You need to direct your anger toward the blameworthy person, the harasser.

Don't Delay Taking Action

If you delay action when someone harasses you, it is likely to continue.

Don't Keep It To Yourself

By being quiet about sexual harassment, you enable it to continue. Chances are extremely good that you are not the only victim. Speaking up can protect other people from also becoming victims. Additionally, not telling anyone encourages feelings of helplessness and can lead to blaming yourself for the incident. If sexual harassment occurs during a co-op assignment, inform your co-op adviser *immediately.*

What You Can Do about Sexual Harassment

Ignoring sexual harassment does not make it go away. Indeed, it may make it worse because the harasser may misinterpret no response to their behavior. Here are some options about how to respond.

- Speak up at the time. Say "no" clearly, firmly, and without smiling. This is not a time to be polite or vague.

- Keep records. A journal noting times, dates, and the types of harassment will help document your experiences. Any letters or notes received should be kept.

- Tell someone. Most employers have an Equal Opportunity Officer in the Human Resources Department. Immediately contact your co-op adviser, a co-worker or the proper person in the chain-of-command. This helps to avoid isolation and the tendency to blame yourself

- Inform someone at the Women's Center or Counseling Services at the college or university. If a female feels uncomfortable talking to a male about this problem, these centers can provide same-sex counselors.

- Try to avoid situations in which you will be alone with the person who is sexually harassing you. Do not put yourself in potentially dangerous situations.

♦ CASE STUDY ♦
Sexual Harassment: Case One

It is Sue's first co-op quarter and she wants to make a good impression. For the first four weeks everything goes well. Then her supervisor is replaced. Her new supervisor begins making comments on how nice she looks. At first she is flattered, but then the supervisor begins making comments with sexual overtones. She is unsure what to do, so she says nothing to these comments. Her supervisor then begins asking her to meet him for a drink after work and implies if she wants to get ahead, this will help. In a polite way, she turns him down. Later he asks her to stay late after work. He begins putting his hands all over her body and making explicit sexual comments. Frightened, she runs out of the office.

Question: What should she do next?

Question: How might she have handled the situation differently?

Question: When do you feel the sexual harassment first took place?

Question: If you were her co-op adviser how would you handle this situation?

♦ CASE STUDY ♦

Sexual Harassment: Case Two

Brenda was a co-op student working for a large corporation. For the last few days she had been working with Mr. Jones to repair a large piece of machinery. Mr. Jones was a consultant for another firm, which was contracted to provide repair services. This is Brenda's story:

On Monday, October 28, 1994, I met with Mr. Jones of QC Corporation. After completing an inspection of the repaired equipment, we came back to the office. Mr. Jones filed his final report and was on his way out of the plant when I happened to mention that I was a co-op student. He asked me what major I was in. I told him Chemical Engineering. He asked me how the guys in my major feel about women in engineering. I told him that I had never heard them say anything about that. He then looked me right in the eye and said, "I don't think women should be in technical fields". Mr. Jones proceeded to tell me how men's brains are superior to women's and that in his experience women don't make good engineers. Looking at me sympathetically he said, "don't take it too hard" and left the plant.

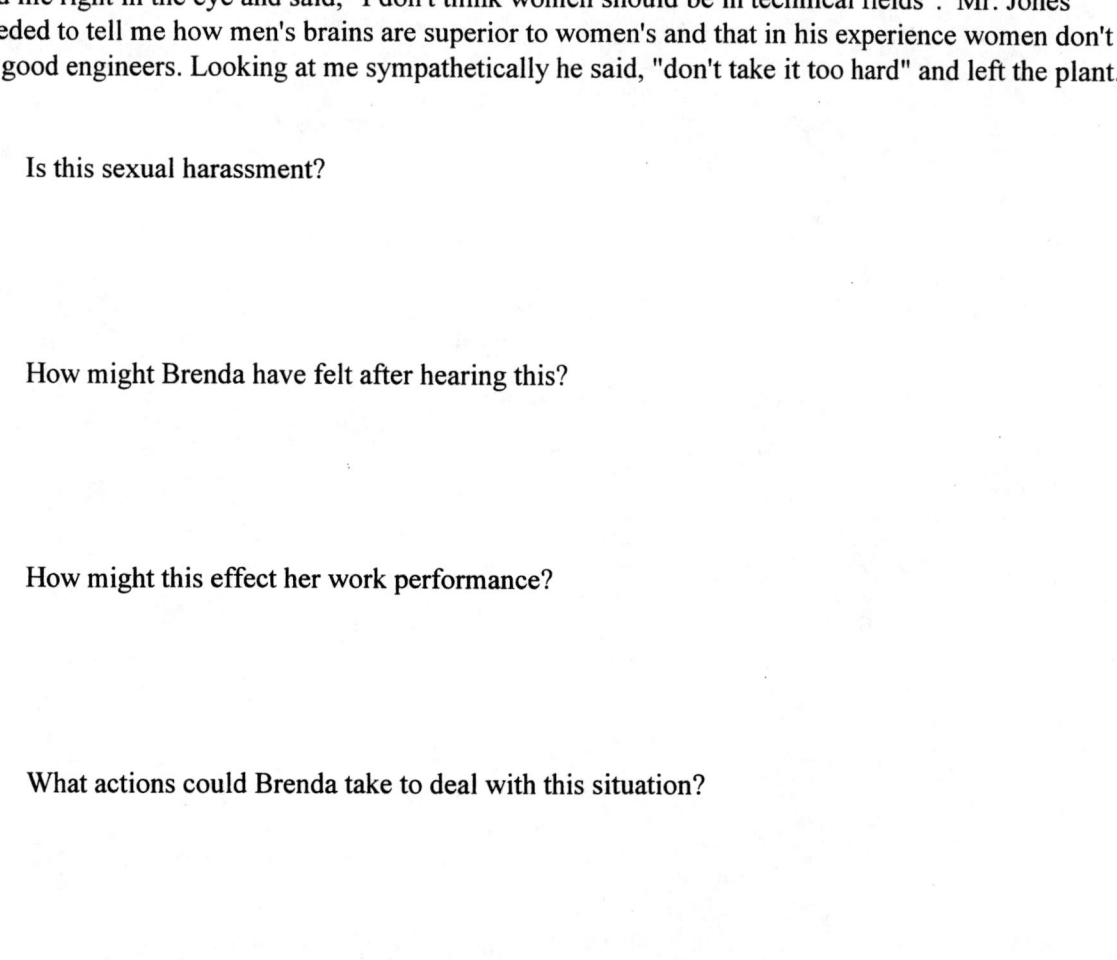

Is this sexual harassment?

How might Brenda have felt after hearing this?

How might this effect her work performance?

What actions could Brenda take to deal with this situation?

How might Mr. Jones' actions escalate to sexual discrimination?

Success is a Journey, not a destination.

–Ben Sweetland

References

Asante, Molefi Kete. *Aftocentricity.* Trenton, NJ: Africa World Press, 1989.

Axtell, Roger E. *Do's and Taboos Around the World.* New York: John Wiley & Sons, 1993.

_____. *The Do's and Taboos of hosting International Visitors.* New York: John Wiley & Sons,1990.

_____. *The Do's and Taboos of international Trade, A Small Business Primer.* New York: John Wiley & Sons, 1991.

Bolles, Richard Nelson. *What Color Is Your Parachute?* Berkeley: Ten Speed Press, 1993.

Bone, Diane. *The Business of Listening: A Practical Guide to Effective Listening.* Los Altos, CA: Crisp Publications, 1988.

Braude, Jacob M. *Complete Speaker's and Toastmaster's Library,* 2nd ed. Englewood Cliffs, NJ: Prentice Hall, 1992.

Brown, H. Jackson, Jr. *Life's Little Instruction Book.* Nashville, TN: Rutledge Hill, 1991.

Carney, C., & Wells, C. *Discover the Career Within You,* 3rd ed. Pacific Grove, CA: Brooks/Cole, 1991.

Farr, J. Michael, Richard Gaither, and R. Michael Pickrell. *The Work Book.* Bloomington, IL: McKnight, 1983.

Fisher, Glen. *Mindsets: The Role of Culture and Perception in International Relations.* Yarmouth, ME: Intercultural Press, 1988.

Gonzalez, Alberto, Marsha Houston, and Victoria Chen. *Our Voices: Essays in Culture, Ethnicity, and Communication, An Intercultural Anthology.* Los Angeles: Roxbury Publishing, 1994.

Hall, Edward, and Meredith Hall. *Hidden Differences.* New York: Anchor Press/Doubleday, 1987.

Keeling, Ann. "Minorities and Cooperative Education" *Journal of Cooperative Education* (Winter 1994), Special Issue on Diversity.

Kimbro, Dennis and Napoleon Hill. *Think and Grow Rich: A Black Choice.* New York: Fawcett Columbine, 1991.

Kohls, Robert L. *Survival Kit for Overseas Living: For Americans Planning to Live and Work Abroad.* Yarmouth, ME: Intercultural Press,1984.

Krannich, C. and R. Krannich. *Interview for Success: A Practical Guide to Increasing Job Interviews, Offers and Salaries.* Woodbridge, VA: Impact Publications, 1990.

Lakein, Alan. *How To Get Control of Your Time and Your Life.* New York: The New American Library, 1973.

Langford, Darnice R. "Dispelling Stereotypes in a Multicultural Co-op Environment. The *Journal of Cooperative Education* (Winter 1994).

Lexicon Publishing. *The New Lexicon Webster's Dictionary of the English Language.* New York: Author, 1991.

Liebling, A. J. *The Most of A.J Liebling.* New York: Simon and Schuster, 1963.

Lindquist, Victor R. *The Northwestern Lindquist-Endicott Report.* Evanston, IL: Northwestern University Placement Center, 1992.

McLuhan, Marshall, and Bruce P. Powers. *The Global Village: Transformations in World Life and Media in the 21st Century.* New York: Oxford University Press, 1989.

Metzler, Ken. *Creative Interviewing.* Englewood Cliffs, NJ: Prentice-Hall, 1977.

Ohio Civil Rights Commission. *Questioning Applicants for Employment and Member in Labor Organizations: A Guide for Application Forms and Interviews,* Columbus, OH: Author, 1994.

Osher, Bill, and Sioux Henley Campbell. *The Blue Chip Graduate: A Four Year College Plan for Career Success.* Atlanta: Peachtree Publishers, 1987.

Park, Clyde W. *Ambassador to Industry: The Idea and Life of Herman Schneider.* Indianapolis: Bobbs-Merrill, 1943.

Powell, C. Randall. *Career Planning & Placement for the College Graduate of the 70s.* Dubuque, IA: Kendall/Hunt, 1974.

_____ *Career Planning Today,* 2nd ed. Dubuque, IA: Kendall/Hunt, 1990.

Reed, Jean. *Resumes That Get Jobs,* 3rd ed. New York: Arco, 1985.

RoAne, Susan. *How To Work a Room-A Guide To Successfully Managing the Mingling.* New York: Shapolsky Books, 1988.

Rouillard, Larrie A. *Goals and Goal Setting.* Menlo Park, CA: Crisp Publications, 1993.

Samovar, Larry A., and Porter, Richard E. *Communication Between Cultures.* Belmont, CA: Wadsworth, 1991.

Scheele, Adele. *Skills for Success,* 4th ed. New York: Ballantine Books, 1983.

Schein, E. H. *Career Dynamics: Matching Individual and Organizational Needs,* Reading, MA: Addison Wesley, 1978.

Simons, George F. *Working Together: How To Become More Effective in a Multicultural Organization.* Los Altos, CA: Crisp Publications, 1989.

Sorenson, Laura. "Tending Friendships Even When Work Gets in the Way," *Working Woman,* October 1987, 108-111.

Stanat, Kirby W., with Reardon, Patrick. *Job Hunting Secrets and Tactics.* Chicago: Follett Publishing, 1977.

Sukiennik, D., L. Raufman, W. Bendat, and Moorpark College. *The Career Fitness Program: Exercising Your Options.* Scottsdale, AZ: Gorsuch Scarisbrick, 1986.

Thompson, Melvin R. *Why Should I Hire You?* Venture Press, 1975.

Wegmann, C. E., and Robert Chapman. *The Right Place at the Right Time: Finding the Right Job in the New Economy.* Berkeley: Ten Speed Press, 1987.

Welch, Mary Scott. *Networking: The Great New Way for Women To Get Ahead.* New York: Harcourt Brace Jovanovich, 1980.

About the Contributors

Vasso Apostolides, Associate Professor of Professional Practice, advises students in the Architecture program and teaches Introduction to Cooperative Education courses to students in the Urban Planning program and in the Colleges of Arts & Sciences and Business Administration. She has conducted research on cooperative education as a discipline and as a method of professional instruction. She holds a Diploma in Architectural Engineering, a M.S. in Urban Planning and a M.S. in Library and Information Science.

Cheryl L. Cates, Associate Professor of Professional Practice, has experience with optional and mandatory programs in a variety of disciplines. She co-authored Learning Outcomes, The Educational Value of Cooperative Education, a book commissioned by the Cooperative Education Association. She served on the Board of Trustees for the Accreditation Council for Cooperative Education. She has received research grants on the state, regional and national level and has presented at numerous professional conferences. She has a B.A. in Public Relations and a Masters in Business Administration.

Marilyn P. Dunn, Associate Professor of Professional Practice is the faculty adviser for Electrical Engineering students. Her teaching experience includes Introduction to Cooperative Education; Business Administration management courses and an Honors Program course at UC; Professional Development Courses as a Visiting Professor in East Africa; 30+ workshops for co-op professionals; and articles published by the Cooperative Education Association and the World Council for Curriculum and Instruction. Her educational background includes a BS in Education and an MBA in Management/Marketing.

John C. Hattendorf, Associate Professor of Professional Practice, serves as faculty adviser to Marketing and Real Estate co-ops. He has served as Secretary and President of the Ohio Cooperative Education Association and in 1997 he was named their Educator Member of the Year. He has previously served as Director of Admissions and Associate Vice Provost for Admissions and Student Services at the University of Cincinnati. He has a B.B.A. in Accounting and a M.Ed. in Administration and Counseling.

Ann E. Keeling, Professor of Professional Practice and former Associate Director in the Division, administers the cooperative education programs for students in Accounting, Finance and Economics. She has held board positions in the national, regional and local cooperative education associations and served on the Editorial Board of the Journal of Cooperative Education. She co-authored a chapter, *College-to-Career Transition Programs for Multiethnic Students* in the book, The Senior Year Experience. She holds a BS in Education, a MS in Special Education and dual Specialists Certificates in Learning Disabilities and Mental Retardation.

Darnice R. Langford, Associate Professor of Professional Practice, advises and places business and engineering students. She has published and presented on various co-op topics including diversity and learning outcomes for WACE, the Illinois/Indiana Section of ASEE, CEA, OCEA and the Journal of Cooperative Education. Chair of the Curriculum Committee, she co-wrote and led the effort to develop a co-op textbook titled "Professional Practice: A Student Text/Workbook Designed to Enhance the Cooperative Education Experience." She holds a BS and an MBA.

Brenda J. LeMaster, Professor of Professional Practice and Vice Provost. Prof. LeMaster has worked with students in Electrical, Mechanical, Industrial, Metallurgical, and Materials Engineering, and students in Accounting, Communications and English. She is past chair of the Cooperative Education Division of the American Society for Engineering Education and a founding board member of the Accreditation Council for Cooperative Education. She hold a B.A. in English and an M.A. in Communications.

Cynthia Lockhart, Associate Professor of Professional Practice, she is responsible for the cooperative education program for students majoring in Fashion Design and Product Development/Merchandising in the College of Design, Architecture, Art and Planning. Cynthia teaches, Introduction to Cooperative

Education, Portfolio Design and Travel Trend Design Seminars in Italy. As a fashion designer and artist, she is the recipient of numerous honors and awards. She has a B. S. in Design and Masters in Design.

Sandra M. McGlasson, Associate Professor of Professional Practice. She is responsible for the cooperative education program for students majoring in graphic design in the College of Design, Architecture, Art, and Planning. She has held administrative positions within the Division, most recently serving as the Interim Director. As a practicing graphic designer, she has been a recipient of numerous local and national professional awards. She has a BS in design.

Thomas M. Newbold, Associate Professor of Professional Practice, teaches cooperative education courses and is the Professional Practice Professor for Civil and Environmental Engineering students. Tom was Past President of the Ohio Cooperative Education Association and Educator Member of the Year. Tom has also been active in the Cooperative Education Association, the Cooperative Education Division of ASEE, the Midwest Cooperative Education Association and the Cooperative Education Network. He has an A.S. in Industrial Management, B.S. and M.Ed. in Education.

Armand Re, former Associate Professor of Professional Practice, was the cooperative education adviser to Industrial Design and Graphic Design Students. He has a B.S. in Art Education and a M.S. in Industrial Design.

E. Sam Sovilla, Professor of Professional Practice, served as Associate Provost and Director of the Division of Professional Practice from 1975 to 2000. His professional activities have included twelve published articles, president and chair of both national co-op professional associations and the state association, on-site consultant for 36 colleges and over 100 presentations at professional conferences nationally and internationally. He has received numerous professional recognitions, including renaming two organizational awards for member excellence in his name. He holds a BA, MA and Certificate in Business Administration.

Louis W. Trent is an Associate Professor and Assistant Director in the Division of Professional Practice. He administers the cooperative education program for mechanical engineering students and is responsible for a variety of administrative duties within the Division. Dr. Trent is past-president and Educator Member of the Year of the Ohio Cooperative Education Association and has served on state, regional and national cooperative education committees. He has a Ph.D. in Counseling Psychology.

Brenda Krueger Wilson, former Associate Professor of Professional Practice, administered the cooperative education programs for Computer Engineering and Electrical Engineering students. She has a B.A. in Communication Arts and a M.A. in Communication and Business Management.